CREATE

MAIJA FAST

CRACK THE CAST –
BECOME THE CREATIVE LEADER
YOU WANT TO BE

Copyright© 2023 Maija Fast

Published by Known Publishing, 2023

The right of Maija Fast to be identified as the Author
of the Work has been asserted by her in accordance
with the Copyright, Designs and Patents Act 1988.
All rights reserved.

Paperback: 978-1-915850-02-7

Hardback: 978-1-915850-06-5

Ebook: 978-1-915850-03-4

This book is sold subject to the condition it shall not, by way of trade or
otherwise, be circulated in any form or by any means, electronic or otherwise
without the publisher's prior consent.

WWW.GET-KNOWN.CO.UK

Maija gently guides the reader towards bravely discovering their inner (maybe even hidden?) creativity ... The bravery and vulnerability she demonstrates by sharing very personal content makes this book particularly inspiring.

Rina Sirén – Partner, Program Director, Miltton Sparks

Creativity and curiosity have never been more needed... This book helps all of us to become truly creative leaders in all aspects of our lives. Thank you Maija for giving us this beautiful book.

Mark Manley – Executive, Leadership and Team Coach

This book is incredibly important. It is the kind of deep dive into oneself that every one of us should do despite the role we have... Everything that Maija writes shines through courage, professionalism and a life lived with her heart.

Riikka Seppälä – Dare to Lead Facilitator by Brené Brown, Leadership and Emotional Skills Coach

Maija's book is full of vivid stories that bring the reader immense joy whilst also making them reflect upon leadership and learning through challenged thinking.

Visa Randell – Tax Director, Chairman of the Board

Maija Fast has written a leadership book for our time. Whether you are in a corporate environment or community, entrepreneur or on a mission to live a richer, freer and more creative life, this book is for you!

**Stacia Keogh – Speaker and Story Coach,
Host of *Finding My Voice* podcast**

Reading this book has totally changed my view about what creativity really is and how it can be harnessed and applied.

**Guy How – Violin-maker, Entrepreneur,
Owner of How Violins**

To Ebba, Eelis and Oliver.

You inspire me to strive towards
creating a bright tomorrow.

CONTENTS

ABOUT MAIJA FAST	9
GUEST WRITERS	11
THIS BOOK IS FOR	15
A CALL FOR CREATIVITY	17
THIS BOOK WILL CRACK YOUR CAST	21
HOW TO USE THIS BOOK	27
FOREWORD	31

Chapter 1
PASSION FOR CREATIVITY — 35

Chapter 2
MAKING MAGIC HAPPEN IN EVERYDAY LIFE — 61

Chapter 3
CRACKING THE MYTHS — 77

Chapter 4
THE CREATE FRAMEWORK — 85

Chapter 5
CURIOSITY — 115

Chapter 6
RESPECT YOURSELF AND OTHERS (WILL TOO) — 141

Chapter 7
EASE AND EFFORTLESSNESS — 173

Chapter 8
ATTITUDE 203

Chapter 9
TAKE OPPORTUNITIES 233

Chapter 10
ENABLE – BE THE CREATIVE LEADER 259

CONCLUSIONS: DID YOU CRACK THE CAST? 297
A HUMBLE THANK YOU TO MY CREATIVE FAMILY 305
MEET THE AUTHOR 311
BIBLIOGRAPHY 315
ENDNOTES 321

ABOUT MAIJA FAST

Maija Fast is the author behind Create. She is an inspirational enabler, catalyst and connector seeing possibilities everywhere. Her multidisciplinary work internationally addresses the needs and potential of human creativity.

She gathers together passionate people with varied skill sets to create something unique.

In her roles as a mother, speaker, gallerist and community activist, as well as in her work as a coach and leader, she focuses on listening and supporting. Maija is a facilitator of growth, noticing elements within and coaxing out the creativity innate in all of us.

Maija has held several leadership positions, been part of seven leadership teams and has led networks and associations for more than 20 years in multiple fields and organisations both internationally and in her native Finland.

GUEST WRITERS

ESTÈVE PANNETIER
Communication Anthropologist, Co-founder of Green Elephant

CASPER MOLTKE-LETH
Partner and board member at law firm Bird & Bird Global; Country Manager, Bird & Bird Denmark

BRANDO LOUHIVAARA
Innovator, Business Designer, Creative Leader

HELENE AURAMO
CEO, Founder of multiple start-ups (e.g. SLUSH and Prönö)

TUOMAS YLÄ-ANTTILA
Associate Professor of Political Science, University of Helsinki

SAANA ROSSI
Author, Advisor, Speaker, ex-HR Director

STEPHANIE AITKEN
Women's Leadership Coach and Trainer

HILKKA-MAIJA KATAJISTO

Partner Workplace Nordic, HR Director

HELI BACKMAN

Organisational Energy Consultant, Executive and Leadership Coach, Co-Founder and Podcast Host

CAMILLA TUOMINEN

Emotion Trainer, Author of five books about Leading Emotions, Keynote Speaker

RIIKKA PAJUNEN

Coach, Author, Entrepreneur Montevista

RAJKUMAR SABANADESAN

Leadership Consultant, former child soldier

LIISA HOLMA

CEO Un-known, Author, Podcast Host

KIMMO RÖNKÄ

CEO, Future Living Specialist, Neighbourhood Designer, Founder of the Kannelmäki Movement

SIAMÄK NAGHIAN

CEO, Genelec

CREATE

CRACK THE CAST –

BECOME THE CREATIVE LEADER

YOU WANT TO BE

THIS BOOK IS FOR

People-oriented leaders who want to use their creativity to encourage their teams to perform at their best but find themselves in situations where creativity is not fully valued or supported.

You may even feel like you've had to hide it to fit in or you've been fearful of being judged by embracing it and being different.

You want to be your authentic self as a leader but keep finding yourself having to conform.

You do not need to have a leadership title to be a creative leader. By harnessing your creativity you can become an inspiring leader in all areas of your life: work, family, friendships and community.

This book is for you if you are creative but feel that you cannot utilise your creativity to its full extent in business.

I'm talking to you if you are constantly battling and feeling unappreciated for being yourself.

Consider these questions:

- Do you feel that you have more to give than your organisation is ready for?

- Have you been told that you have too many ideas?

- Do you feel like you have to hide part of yourself to gain value?

- Are you frustrated that day-to-day creativity and innovation is not championed even though it is supposed to be a strategic objective?

- Have you changed jobs many times only to see that the same old problems and patterns repeat?

- Do you want to be able to be your genuine self at work and embrace your strengths?

- Do you wish you could get your team with you on the creative journey?

If you answered "yes" to any of these questions, I wrote this book for you.

Please know that you are not alone. I also once answered "yes" to most of them too. I have spent the last 15 years finding the answers for myself and helping people just like you to thrive as authentic leaders and creative human beings.

A CALL FOR CREATIVITY

"The only unique contribution that we will ever make in this world will be born of our creativity."

[1]**BRENÉ BROWN**

WHY IS THERE A NEED FOR CREATIVITY IN LEADERSHIP?

The world is full of uncertainty. We need our leaders to think and act differently as we tackle increasingly difficult issues. What got us here won't get us where we need to be. We need a new type of leader. A creative one!

Creativity helps you to navigate and embrace uncertainty. The kind of creativity I am talking about is people-oriented and compassionate. It takes into account everybody's strengths and differing capabilities. At the same time it involves business understanding. It is about having an open mindset and being brave enough to take chances; think and act outside the box.

The era of hard leadership is over. The brave leader of today is compassionate, vulnerable and inclusive.

WHY DOES THIS NEED CHANGING NOW?

All the lists of the skills that will be required for the future of work highlight creativity, yet it is not appropriately valued in business today. We live in a time where machines are taking over the majority of routine work, but there are still certain things that only humans can do. This will become increasingly important in the future, and it is our responsibility to light the way for the coming generations.

WHAT IS THE COST OF NOT DOING IT?

We will have stagnated companies full of underperforming and unhappy people who are not utilising their potential.

Businesses that do not embrace creativity now will be replaced by the competition and have no place in the future economy.

On a global scale, we need creativity to think of ways of working and producing in a more sustainable way to protect the planet we live on.

The stakes are high!

WHY IS IT YOUR RESPONSIBILITY TO DO SOMETHING ABOUT IT?

We are all responsible. Every one of us has the power and ability to influence and inspire others through creativity. You can be the catalyst in your community, organisation and with the people closest to you. You do not necessarily need to have a position or a role as a leader to lead and engage people around you.

Be open, be the change.

THIS BOOK WILL CRACK YOUR CAST

This book shifts creatives and leaders from feeling inadequate and wrong to the point where they can see their strengths to a place of self-knowledge and respect, whilst keeping an open mindset. It can lure out your creativity if you have been fighting against it or are sitting with a fixed mindset and believe you are not creative.

This book will challenge you to find your own personal kind of creativity. When you get there, you will be ready to enable and lead others creatively by respecting the strengths of others and seeing endless opportunities.

Once you have read this book:

1. You will find your own way of being creative, and you will be able to use this in your work and your life as a

whole. You will be on the path to becoming a creative leader!

2. You will recognise that you have something special to give your community and organisation. You will feel respected and valued for being you, and you will operate from a place where you have integrated the different parts of you and your life into one creative playing field.

3. You will have a better picture of how you want to write the story of your life. You will feel free to not act upon other people's expectations but to instead set up your own kind of CREATE career and control the telling of the story of your life.

I have a principle that everything I do needs to feel that it gives more than it takes. When you have the tools, it will be an easy flow going forward. It doesn't mean that everything goes smoothly and the road is free of bumps. It is about the attitude of seeing growth possibilities, even during the hard bits. Creating an enjoyable life even when the circumstances are not ideal. The reality is that even when it is light there are shadows. What matters is how you relate to them.

You may have tried to fit into a certain form and felt that it didn't work for you. Cracking the Cast refers to a mould or a role that you try to fit in. Now is the time to break loose from expectations and live a life that looks and feels like your own. The purpose of this book is to give creativity and creative people the value they deserve in business life.

It is interesting how little creativity seems to be valued in business, even though it is set as a strategic priority in many organisations. Every organisation wants to be innovative, but most organisations' cultures don't feed curiosity, innovation or risk-taking. You will learn if your organisation is supporting an open mindset and curiosity or not. You can be the one to start the change, together with the people around you.

Curiosity and creativity belong to everyone. They are not owned by a group of especially artistic people. When we invite creativity into our lives they become much more interesting. In moments when you have failed with the execution of a task or received critical feedback, it is hard to find the power of curiosity. It is easy to shrink and be affected by the feedback. However, instead of beating yourself up and wanting to vanish from the scene, look at it curiously. Why did that happen? What can I learn from it? How was the feedback I received influenced by the experiences and the understanding of the giver of the feedback? What does it say about me? Or does it actually tell me more about the giver of the feedback?

This book will teach you what your creativity is made of and support you to find respect for yourself and your strengths to help others to respect you too. This book may change how you think and feel, both about yourself and your colleagues and family members. You can have a huge impact on your surroundings when you know yourself and your strengths and use them creatively. The impact is even bigger when you inspire and enable others to create too. You will see the value of embracing your creativity and you can help both individuals and organisations to thrive. Leadership is a behaviour as [2]Amy Edmondson says. You do not need to have an official role to be leading creativity in your organisation and surroundings.

I am walking through this journey of creative leadership with you, using the CREATE® model that I crafted to help people and organisations open up to their innovativeness. I have also invited interesting people whom I admire to write comments related to the themes of the book. You can find texts by fifteen incredible guest writers: Estève Pannetier, Casper Moltke-Leth, Brando Louhivaara, Helene Auramo, Tuomas Ylä-Anttila, Saana Rossi, Stephanie Aitken, Hilkka-Maija Katajisto, Heli Backman, Camilla Tuominen, Riikka Pajunen, Rajkumar Sabanadesan, Liisa Holma, Kimmo Rönkä and Siamäk Naghian. These texts can be read as complementing parts of my book or as independent comments relating to the respective themes. Most of these people, I have worked with during my versatile career; others were open and curious enough to participate in the book without knowing me in advance.

Additionally, I am thankful to Rina Sirén, Mark Manley, Riikka Seppälä, Visa Randell, Stacia Keogh, Kay Daniels and Guy How, who have read my book, commented on it and written testimonials. I am very grateful to all of them for giving their time to contribute to my book, joining me on the revolution of giving creativity and creative people the value they deserve.

My mission is to both empower you and to help you empower others. The CREATE framework is convenient in the sense that it helps you to help yourself and others at the same time. The outcome: a more confident you. A leader who believes they have something unique to give. Through your new level of confidence and by focusing on your strengths, you can achieve incredible results for yourself, your team and your organisation.

> *"Be yourself; everyone else is already taken."*
>
> **OSCAR WILDE**

HOW TO USE THIS BOOK

After completing the first draft of this book I gave it to a number of people to see what impact it would have on them. Their words serve as a great guide to how to get the most out of this book.

LET GO OF YOUR "I'M NOT CREATIVE" LIMITING BELIEF

Guy How (violin-maker and entrepreneur) read this book and surprised himself: "I've been working with Maija both personally and professionally for a number of years now. She often told me that I was very creative, but I had never seen it.

"Reading this book has totally changed my view about what creativity really is and how it can be harnessed and applied… Creativity can be an attitude, an approach that uses your current set of skills in a new way by answering the right questions."

WITH A CHANGEMAKING MINDSET

Rina Sirén's (a partner at consultancy firm Miltton Sparks) mindset changed when she read this book: "I started reading CREATE with a logical mindset. Then I checked in with myself and asked: what if the whole point is to let go of logic and discover my inner (maybe even hidden) creativity?

"So, I tossed that out of the window, which had a transformative effect.

"I had to let go of my 'I'm not a creative' belief in order to gain the assurance and confidence that even I have lots of creativity to tap into. What a liberating reading experience!

"You can either read the book as a thought-provoking but light read, or you can choose to do the exercises and get sucked into an introspective and transformative process."

USE THE MODEL

The CREATE® model consists of Curiosity, Respect Yourself and Others (will too), Ease and effortlessness, Attitude and acceptance, Take opportunities, and Enable. To become the full-blown Creative Leader you need to tap into all of these fields. But you can start leading creatively right away. Every individual has different strengths and needs to develop further in different areas. You will find out what your needs are.

In Chapter 1 I will introduce you to where we stand in the world with leadership and creativity, and where we are heading. I will also give a voice to my guest writers going forward. There are fifteen professionals, from lawyers and leadership coaches to professors and authors, bringing their insights and expertise to the book. In Chapter 2 I'll tell my growth story to becoming a creative leader. In Chapter 3 I'll open up the myths that keep us from advancing into creative leadership. Chapter 4 introduces the CREATE model in depth and Chapters 5-10 allow you to dive deeper into each area of the model. You can choose to read the book chronologically or dive deeper into the sections that interest you the most.

Picture 1. The CREATE circle - simple model

DO THE ACCOMPANYING EXERCISES

Each Chapter of the CREATE model contains exercises to help you find out what your kind of creativity is and how to bring that into your life and leadership. You can download the CREATE workbook at www.fastcreative.ninja/workbook/ and find a template for deepening your journey. Be ready to look yourself in the mirror to take your team, community and organisation with you to the next level.

Your journey starts now.

FOREWORD

WAR AND LOVE AND CARELIAN PIE

While I was writing this book, Russia started a war against Ukraine on 24 February 2022. It made me doubt the meaningfulness of writing about something so light and idealistic as creative leadership. It brought my thoughts back to my grandparents who were both born in 1917, the same year Finland became independent after having spent a long time under Russian or Swedish rule. Ukraine is not a neighbouring country to Finland, but what we have in common is a long border with Russia.

My grandparents – Eeva, from Finnish Carelia (which is now part of Russia), and Swedish Finnish Nils, from the west coast of Finland – both spent five years of their youth at war, from 1939 to 1944. My grandfather was a soldier and my grandmother a nurse. They saw horrible things. My grandfather's brother never came home from the front line.

At the front line, Eeva and Nils also found love. They met each other in the field hospital when Eeva removed a shot from Nils's buttock. A shot he got when he was duck hunting in the woods with his friends. Ironically, he was shot on the front line whilst duck hunting. Eeva roasted the duck for Nils, and they fell in love.

Nils never spoke about the war again, not until almost half a century later when he spoke to me. He told how he was taken hostage by the Russians. They asked him what his profession was and he answered that he had a diploma in economics, and he was rescued because they thought he was a diplomat. It didn't go as well for his friends who were shot.

My grandmother, who had seen war and shortage, always cooked with butter and cream. She didn't like the company of old people because she thought that they only talked about diseases and dead people. She did not want Carelia back. Every week she baked cinnamon rolls for her family to get her children and grandchildren to visit her. She believed that I could do anything.

When Russia attacked Ukraine, I felt numb. It brought back the stories from my family's history and I started questioning whether there was any justification for writing a book about creative leadership at a time like this. Is it naive to think that we can create happy organisations and thriving people when there are more important things to think about?

I was thinking about my grandmother who wanted to enjoy life in her way and who believed in me. I thought that now was exactly the right time to see light where we can see light. It is important to be human and humane to each other. It is important to raise our voices and not accept what is happening. If everything is enveloped by our fear of war, Putin wins.

Let us give space in this time for the development of people and organisations, psychological safety and all the things that can be real in open and respectful societies. Let's still work on the small things. It doesn't take away the importance of the big things. It makes us human beings. It makes us happier.

Rajkumar Sabanadesan, who has been both a child soldier in Sri Lanka and a refugee in Finland, told me that creative leadership is crisis leadership to him. Rajkumar says: "Ideology is important, values are important, principles are important, but creativity is more important when dealing with a crisis." Let's be creative. Let's have hope and build a better world.

When my grandmother Eeva died, I found her memory books where her friends had written memories to her before she left to go to war. A friend wrote to her: "Keep your humour. It is disinfectant". That is so beautiful. The humour of a nurse on the front line has to be disinfectant. Finding the lightness even in hard times helps us to keep moving forward; creativity is not only nice to have but critical.

I know my grandmother would be proud of me for writ-ing this book. And she would definitely show the finger to Putin and eat her delicious Carelian pie, with a lot of butter.

Lure out the creativity in you! Thank you for being on this path with me.

Maija

AUTHOR OF CREATE

Crack the Cast –

Become the Creative Leader You Want to Be

CHAPTER 1

PASSION FOR CREATIVITY

"If you wish that the world around you would be more gracious, softer, more creative, calmer, more genuine or sensitive... dare to be that yourself."

BY KATRI SYVÄRINEN

CREATIVITY IS A MINDSET

I wrote this book to grant creativity and creative people the value they deserve in business life. Creativity is mentioned in all lists of most important future working skills and yet it is, in my experience, undervalued in business organisations. Every organisation claims to be innovative, but are the cultures of these organisations supporting innovation? I would like to see more innovation and creativity in workplaces. A lot of knowledge and skills are underused when people try to be something they are not. I want to also find the people who think that they are not creative but will become so much more when they dare to look their hidden creativity in the eyes. When you get the real strengths of people being used, both people and organisations thrive. I want to show the value of embracing your creativity. You can have a huge impact on your surroundings when you know yourself and your strengths and use them creatively. The impact is even bigger when you inspire and enable others to create too. In this Chapter, I will introduce to you where we stand in the world with leadership and creativity, and where we are heading.

The World Economic Forum is forecasting that it is more and more important for the future of work that we learn skills that help us to manage in times of uncertainty, as Camilla Tuominen[4] highlights in her book about leading emotions. She says that creativity and making connections are the key, as well as the reading of silent signals and emotional skills that help us to navigate in uncertain circumstances. According to Tuominen, "In the future, machines are delivering and people are connecting and creating."

Futurist [5]Perttu Pölönen says that some of the most important skills in the future will be curiosity and experimenting, creativity and improvisation, problem solving skills, passion and character, communication and storytelling, self-knowledge and moral bravery, to mention a few. All of these are elements of creativity, reflecting the way I see creativity as a wide phenomenon and mindset.

Creativity is not something soft and fluffy but a hardcore skill that provides organisations with innovative solutions. It is a working tool among other tools. You just have to use your creativity consciously to be able to use it fully or find your way of being creative if you have not recognised it yet.

Creativity can be expressed through painting or music or in other artistic ways, but creativity is not art – it is a mindset.

It is also not something that you have or do not have. You can practise using your creativity and become the spark that your surroundings or organisation needs to blossom and succeed.

I am not just reaching out to people in creative fields but putting new focus on those who are working in fields that are not usually seen as creative. Afterall, the impact is huge when you can embed curiosity and a creative mindset into the fields that are not naturally seen as creative. I am talking to all of you who can see that you would have more to give if you could just dare to unleash your imagination. We have a lot of people in our business organisations who feel that they are not respected for who they are and they are instead hiding their real strengths so they can be valued.

Understanding opposite views is empathy and creates openness, giving you the chance to understand the world around you rather than sitting in your own kind of sandbox, no matter how creative you may be within it. New things are born in friction. Hence, it is very dangerous when social media networks like Facebook offer a picture of the world for their users that is only representing everybody's own bubble. Even educated people may end up thinking and feeling that their view is the world view.

It is not very helpful to bring some form of art into the business world and claim that doing this would help the leadership. If a leadership team suddenly starts painting, it doesn't make their leadership better. They may have moments of reflection and get insights while painting, but to actually make an impact, creativity needs to be integrated into your business.

The creativity that I am talking about involves business understanding. It is about having an open mindset and seeing possibilities. It is about being brave enough to take chances and think and act outside the box. According to [6]Teresa M. Amabile "In business, it is not enough for an idea to be original – the idea must also be useful, appropriate and functional. It must somehow influence how the business gets done."

How do you ideate out of the box in a way that it brings something new and valuable to the table? What helps greatly with that is to not fear. Organisations with psychological safety are braver and more creative. [7]Amy Edmondson has studied psychological safety already for decades. She says that psychological safety is not only a nice to have, but mission critical. She gives examples from the hospital world where lives have been saved or lost because of psychological safety vs. the lack of it. Everybody's voice is critical. If people do not dare to speak up, we can lose lives as well as businesses. Edmondson also says that diversity in itself doesn't bring more creativity or success to organisations, but diversity with psychological safety does. There can be pockets of innovation also in organisations that are not encouraging innovation, but how can we encourage these pockets of innovation to make the change that is required?

Guest Writer

ESTÈVE PANNETIER

*Communication Anthropologist,
Co-founder of Green Elephant*

Every tension is an opportunity for innovation. What often hinders creativity is avoiding conflict. Especially in countries like Finland where we avoid conflict, people might not dare to create due to fear of conflict. When people understand the difference between "bad" (dysfunctional) conflicts which destroy trust – and "good" (functional) conflicts, they can dance with the tension. It can lead to uncomfortable conversations but paves the way for creativity. The shift from blaming to talking about underlying needs opens immense possibilities. Creativity is a reward from tackling conflict in a constructive way.

[8]Gary Hamel and Michele Zanini say in their book *Humanocracy* that human beings are resilient and inventive but organisations are not. They claim that we have ended up with organisations that lack courage, creativity and passion because that is all we have ever known. They are wondering how companies with billion dollar R&D programmes, celebrity CEOs and access to the best consultants can fail. Many organisations try to not make any mistakes; hence they do not advance according to the future needs. For all their accomplishments, our organisations are inertial, incremental and uninspiring. We tell ourselves that the nature of large organisations is to be backward looking, and to wish otherwise is naive.

Hamel and Zanini suggest that organisations are not innovative and flexible due to the fact that they are less human. According to them, it seems that human-built organisations have room for courage, intuition, love, playfulness and artistry. They think that we shouldn't have to content ourselves with organisations that are authoritarian and joyless. They call on us to confront the inhumanity in organisations and to join a management revolution. We are on the same path trying to humanise the organisations and leadership. As Hamel and Zanini suggest, human beings deserve more from their jobs, and together we can create more dynamic and inventive institutions going forward.

The [9]Deloitte Insights research about social enterprises highlights that, as the business environment becomes more competitive and digital disruption continues, organisations have become more team-centric, networked and agile. They see that this is happening in many functions, such as sales and operations, but according to the respondents the lack of this in C-suite teams was seen as the most pressing human capital issue facing organisations today. There is a huge need for the C-suites to change from being individual C-level experts towards operating as a team. This is called a "symphonic C-suite".

Our CREATE avatar, who is walking with you through this process, is Anna. She is not representing one human being but is a mixture of many clients, colleagues and acquaintances that I have come across during my career. Anna represents a leader who is struggling to find and fight her way through today's business world. She wants to see change around her but finds obstacles on her path. Anna will walk you through this path of creative leadership.

You will read a lot of stories in this book. Some of the stories may be mixed so as to not make people recognisable; if I open up a private story where people can be recognised, it is only if I have their permission to do so. Through reading these stories you may notice that your own story is far more interesting than you imagined. [10]Glennon Doyle writes in her book *Untamed* that she finally asked herself what she wanted for herself rather than what the world wanted from her.

What is the story of your life that you want to write?

My target is to help you to create magic from the everyday and to be the change your organisation needs. You don't need to change yourself. You don't need to travel around the world to find inspiring experiences. It is about being aware, observing and finding. It is about taking action. You can change your mindset and start creating magic in your life and surroundings right now.

Guest writer

CASPER MOLTKE-LETH

Partner and board member at law firm Bird & Bird Global; Country Manager, Bird & Bird Denmark

Lawyers have always been very traditionalist and risk averse, meaning innovation has been considered with scepticism and even anxiousness. Many times innovation as a concept can become problematic if the innovation is or becomes a goal instead of a tool. Many lawyers will freeze (and slightly panic) if they are asked to "innovate".

Therefore, innovation needs to be de-mystified. And it is better to not always be too ambitious. In my view, the innovator is simply the person who questions ways of doing things, but instead of just criticising and then expecting others to do something about it, the innovator actually acts to find a solution. They try to find the new or optimised way to do something. That can be small things, such as tweaking processes or procedures, all the way up to larger projects inventing whole new business concepts and delivery methods. However, all of them are equally important, as many small tweaks can result in a massive change. Therefore, when we want our organisation to innovate, we simply have to teach them to criticise all they want, but also animate them to come up with a suggested solution. So we can do things a little bit better next time.

CREATIVITY IN CRISIS TIMES

I have heard many people say that creativity was killed when people were forced to remote work during the pandemic. Yet my own experience was that my creativity was my number one asset whilst navigating with inaccurate and severely limited information.

I made a poll on LinkedIn in June 2021 asking how people perceived their creativity had been influenced by the new situation with lockdown and forced remote work. The answers were a) My creativity has flourished 52%, b) It remained the same 31%, c) I have not been as creative 15% and d) Creativity was killed 2%. This was not a huge sampling, but according to my LinkedIn connections, there was some evidence to suggest that they felt their creativity was not killed.

This poll was done when the pandemic had lasted over a year already. We experienced almost another year more of it, with ups and downs, hope and backlashes, before the world opened up more and the pandemic changed to an endemic. Then, when the world was finally starting to stabilise, the war broke out in Ukraine.

People were exhausted by the Covid restrictions and just hanging on and finally seeing the light at the end of the tunnel. Then a crisis of a different calibre appeared uninvited in our lives: the war in Ukraine. How well will people manage to maintain their creativity during a crisis that is of a very different kind? The pandemic was a common threat for humankind, even if corona also has been dividing friends and families who have had contrasting approaches to the restrictions. In war, we have different enemies. Even if the war doesn't spread out more broadly, the whole of Europe is facing an energy crisis this winter.

How we manage to overcome the new threats and violations remains to be seen. One thing that is sure, though, is that creativity and an open mindset are very helpful when facing crises. It is known that during wars in the past, different forms of art and creativity have been sources of hope and survival. As mentioned before, Rajkumar Sabanadesan, who has also lived through war, has experienced that creativity is the most important feature during crisis times. Historian [11]Rutger Bregman has been studying human nature. He claims that the previously popular view of us human beings being naturally selfish is turning out to be wrong. He says that, according to research, when a crisis or catastrophe hits, 90% of the people help each other. He says that we are living in a time where the friendliest survive. The leadership models and leadership ideals are also shifting. It is starting to be respected to be a vulnerable, sensitive and creative leader who sees the strengths of the people surrounding them. Helping others to thrive might be our true nature as human beings, and, according to Bregman, there is widespread evidence of this more optimistic view of humanity within research from different academic disciplines.

CRACKS IN THE CAST

Have you been told that you have great ideas, but you could share them less frequently? That has happened to many of my coachees and there are plenty of these stories. Do you feel that people want your energy and get excited about your ideas, but when it comes to changing the current ways of working, or the norms, they get scared and start fighting against it or putting down your ideas? Change might feel exciting in theory, but when it is a potential threat to the status quo or someone's position, the resistance begins. How do you overcome these situations? We will look into that later in the book.

Have you changed jobs many times and felt that you didn't really belong anywhere? Or do you feel wrong because you are not acting as would be natural for you, but instead acting as you feel you are expected to act in your role or your organisation? You might be so used to trying to fit into the cast that you have forgotten your true nature. Acting against your values might be very painful for you. You may even feel it as physical pain or anxiety.

I have news for you: you are the change. You do not need to be a cultural fit. Be the cultural add instead. Once you know yourself well enough and value your skills and want to develop further, your skills will be valued by others too. It is a process. It requires resilience. It requires courage and vulnerability, but I will walk you through the journey.

We have a strong desire for belonging which sometimes makes us behave in ways that are not natural for us. We act like the chameleons of working life. When I was working with a finance team as their HR, I noticed that they were talking about themselves as stereotypes of finance people. I challenged them and said, "I don't believe you. You are human beings with different motivations and different ways of working. What do you burn for? What motivates you?"

In a leadership team that I worked with, most of the team had very fact-based and number-based ways of working. There was one younger woman who had desperately tried to fit into the team and acted as she thought she should so she could be respected. When we did the Enneagram personality tests with the leadership team, and she noticed that her personality was a seven – meaning an energetic innovator – she seemed so relieved. She realised that she was an innovator and change maker and her greatest assets were different to the others, and it wasn't a bad thing. She started to see the value of being herself instead of trying to be a lame version of someone else.

Young people and new people in organisations often have a lot of ideas, and they want to change the ways of working. Surprisingly soon, we get used to the ways of working, becoming blinded to the need for change and for us to renew ourselves and the organisation. Middle management start to look more like copies of each other and act as they think they should. I am exaggerating a bit, but this is how the big picture appears according to my empirical evidence based on many international organisations and from the stories of my coachees.

You are, or you can become, a creative leader when you believe in the power of you and your creativity. The further up the ladder you are, the more you might doubt yourself. Know that imposter syndrome is common. We all have our doubts, that's what makes us grow further, but don't let the doubts paralyse you. You have all the answers in you. Reading this book shows that you already have cracks in the cast. You might have fought out of the stereotypical cast already, or you may need support in doing so, but you are setting yourself on the path towards inspiring others to find their own way to lead creativity.

STRIVING TO BECOME THE CREATIVE LEADER YOU WANT TO BE

Let's introduce our avatar, Anna. She is representing a lot of creative people in organisations that do not see the value of creativity. She is a leader in an organisation that is not particularly known for its creativity. She has a strong passion for people and for making a positive change. She has a clear vision of how the organisation should change, and she drives change which she thinks will bring not only well-being to the organisation but also success to the firm.

Anna feels that the organisation doesn't have the readiness for the change she thinks is needed to be able to attract clients and employees in the future. Anna's days are active. She meets many people and she organises events and drives change in different fields.

She gets energy from supporting her team and enabling them to grow. She gets very excited when she gets to ideate and create new things. She is brilliant at that and has many balls in the air all the time. At the same time, she works also with people who seem to be on a mission to shoot down ideas. It creates tension and pressure. Anna is surrounded by both positive vibes and catabolic energy.

Anna is a member of the leadership team of her organisation and she brings her ideas to the table. Some ignore her: they sit behind their laptops, and she isn't sure whether they are listening or reading their emails. She has some people in the team who listen and believe in her, but they do not step up to support her. Others are passive-aggressive and comment: "Why change something that is not broken?" Anna gets frustrated. She knows that she has good points that would bring positive change within the organisation as well as a good reputation among the clients. When she gets home, she is in her head and doesn't have energy for her children. She feels disappointed not only with her colleagues but also with herself. She blames herself for not being a present mother and a partner when she is annoyed and feels frustrated and even angry for not being able to make the change.

What should Anna do to make herself heard? Anna has a good cause, and she wants only the best for the organisation and its people. But she is not quite aware of how she is presenting things. She doesn't know how she is perceived by the rest of the leadership team. Being insecure about herself, she doesn't even believe that she can drive the change.

Anna feels stuck. She thinks that the feeling might change if she changed jobs, but, at the same time, she has experienced this so many times that she starts to feel that it is her fault. The same pattern repeats in every organisation she enters. It is at first exciting and she gets a welcoming start, and when she starts to bring the creative agenda to the table, the resistance begins.

Anna is not alone with her problem. There are many frustrated people in leadership teams and organisations who either hide their true selves to be respected or who try to be themselves and feel that they are not respected for that. Many younger or older women or men leave work feeling disappointed and end up snapping at their partners and children, feeling frustrated and like they have failed.

They are people with a lot of ideas and energy to take them through. They seem a bit weird in the organisations where processes and matters rule and where there isn't space for doing things in a new way. Many people feel comfortable with their routines and want to keep things as they are. Even if they complain about matters, they are not ready to change themselves or their surroundings. This makes driving change difficult for Anna and her peers.

Over the years I have come across these people in multiple organisations in various fields that I have worked in. I could see that the people with the freshest ideas and drive and passion to change were excited first, then they felt defeated and then they moved on. Most probably so they could face the same pattern in a new organisation.

They have been told that the business cannot offer what they want. They have been asked to tell fewer of their ideas. They have been made smaller. There have been attempts to put them into imaginary boxes where they do not fit.

Guest writer

BRANDO LOUHIVAARA

Innovator, Business Designer, Creative Leader

When it comes down to innovation, the Nordic countries are on top of the world. Finland, once the ruler of the global mobile business with Nokia, is, though, in danger of dropping out of the list of the most progressive countries. The speed of innovation is slowing down, which has a negative impact on the national economy. Have Finns lost their inspiration and creativity?

According to a recent survey, the Finnish people are not as engaged with their work as in the other Nordic countries (Gallup 2022). Only 13% of Finns are motivated about what they do. In faster growing, innovative countries the work inspires approximately 20% of the employees. Overall, there seems to be space for growth in organisations for making work more inspiring.

Gary Hamel describes, in his pyramid of human capabilities, that the value creation and engagement go hand in hand. If a company wants to succeed or at least survive in the changing world, organisations need more than just skills and hard work from their employees. The value is created where people are innovative, creative and motivated.

In a study about Finnish leaders from 2017, they found out that the Finnish leadership style is down to earth and modest. The counter of this is that they lack ambition, ways to build a collaborative culture and ability to inspire people. The traditional Finnish leadership style doesn't support the culture of growth that Gary Hamel talks about.

We need to change how leaders think and lead. We need to equip leaders with more human capabilities. We need our leaders to be coaches, facilitators and servant leaders. The new tribe of leaders understands how to build trust, motivation, collaboration and creativity. The very Finnish way of leading needs to expand outside the box.

THE VALUE OF SHAPING A CAST OF YOUR OWN AND THE COST OF NOT DOING IT

The better the employees and the managers know their strengths and motivators, the more success is seen. The better you know the team around you, the stronger you are together. If you are respected for who you are and trusted to do great work, you will want to give your best. If your duties are discussed and planned together so that you can influence your work and do as much as possible of what energises you, you will be motivated to give the best for your team, manager and company. If you know how to compensate for the bits of your work that don't energise you, you will have more energy left for yourself and your nearest and dearest.

If you try to fit people into the cast, you will find in front of you a group that are unmotivated, frustrated, underperforming and who do low quality work – and you will be faced with high staff turnover and expensive re-recruitment and induction costs. On the individual level, it can cost you your career progression, your happiness, even your relationships, if you try to be someone you are not. If you try to fit in, you will never be as good as when you are working with your strengths. Why do you try to fit in when you were born to stand out?

It is very costly for organisations to not use the full potential of their employees. Self-knowledge, and the knowledge of the skills, motivators and drivers for your team members, are very important in creating productive teams and organisations. If people feel that they cannot grow or thrive, they will look for other places to work. It is as much a structural as a leadership problem if you do not focus on using the strengths of the people within your team or organisation. And that will be costly. A new recruitment costs many months' salary, even when you do not use external recruitment partners.

Some organisations will make money anyway, but whether they will be competitive in the future remains to be seen. It is interesting that even if all lists of skills you need for future work include creativity alongside empathy and communication skills, when it comes to business organisations in real life, creativity doesn't seem to be valued.

[12]The Association for Finnish Work completed a research in 2016 to establish an understanding of what employees and employers valued in working life and what were seen as important future working skills. The questionnaire was answered by 1,006 Finns of working age and 613 people representing the top leadership and Human Resources leadership roles. When asked to choose the four most important features or skills in future work, 18% of the employers' representatives and 19% of the employees said that creativity was amongst the four top skills of future working life. When you look more closely into the results, quite a few other highlighted skills are attached to creativity. The will to develop and capability to learn new things (employer 55%/employee 38%), the capability to change and adaptability (employer 45%/employee 38%), being multi-skilled (employer 42%/employee 51%), to mention a few, are in my mind very tightly connected to creativity. Yet the word "creativity" is not used anywhere near

as frequently as it could be when highlighting the four most important skills. It may be that creativity is not seen as broadly or as something naturally combined with the professions people in this questionnaire are talking about.

In my experience, the Finnish and European working cultures value processes and facts. Even if the world has changed, many organisations are led by rules from the Fordian time. Fordism was created in promoting mass production in manufacturing a hundred years ago, but its principles are used in many organisations for leading people still in the 2020s. Not always consciously, but as a way of operating in practice. As we all know, people cannot be led like machines. When leading people we need capabilities like empathy, creativity and communication skills. We need to understand different personalities and know ourselves so well that we can see how others may perceive us. These capabilities are not manifested in processes. You need a human touch. The bit that machines cannot take over.

You may feel a contradiction with your personality at work, as you know you have a lot to give and you can see that you get people excited around you. You have a lot of ideas for improving things. You are ready to roll your sleeves up to make shit happen, but you cannot get everyone on board. Some will be inspired by you and others will put you down. Most people do not have as many ideas as you and they might press the panic button in their minds when you fly too high.

It is both a structural and individual challenge. The ways of working and the principles and rules of organisations do not always give space for your way of leading. Commonly, leaders are driven by a strong target orientation and are motivated by competition. Our avatar, Anna, is also target-oriented, but, for her, it is important to get to the targets with a feeling of ease, together with the people around her. She wants to create win-win situations. Her approach might look light-hearted or too easy for people in her surroundings. In fact, she is working a lot on hitting her targets through collaboration, by inspiring others, by bringing people together, by having fresh ideas that take organisations forward. For someone who likes a systematic and fact-based approach, she might seem fluffy and less scientific when she trusts her intuition and the people around her.

Many organisations look at past results rather than ideating the future.

That is confusing Anna who always looks to the future. She feels that she never really belongs. She is good at adapting and trying to fit in, but it just feels wrong. Anna has done well. She has reached leadership positions, but insecurity is her friend. She feels as if her skills are not the ones needed. At the same time, she knows she has a lot to give. That is always clear when she starts in a new role. And then comes the resistance. It tears her apart. She feels defeated. And then she collects herself and tries again. She tries to find the people who will follow. She tries to find the people who are on the same mission. She gets a lot done, but she feels that she is not respected. She keeps being told that she could drive her ideas less. That she could be quieter and fit in better. The contradiction between her passion to make a big change and the tempo things are progressing at is eating her from inside.

What Anna has tried to do has not given her the success she desires; she keeps feeling wrong, not enough and a failure. When Anna realises her way is not wrong, she feels more confident. She needs to start focusing on what she can bring to the table by doing things her way. Anna has been desperately trying to fit in. She was trying to change herself to do that, but she ended up being a bad version of herself. Anna has a lot to give, but she needs to vocalise that. "I will never be a cultural fit, more of a cultural add. My value for the organisation is bringing in new perspectives. I have a different approach. We might need to have a couple of conversations to reach our common goals and targets, but once we truly listen to each other and respect each other the result is going to be great."

RESULTS WITH EASE

Self-knowledge and maintaining a healthy respect for different personalities and ways of working are key factors in achieving success. If you try to fit in, you will never be the best version of yourself. As long as you keep feeling that you are wrong and try to fit in at the cost of being true to yourself, you will keep failing.

Many organisations try to find a cultural fit when recruiting people. You are capable of adjusting your style. You can be the chameleon who changes according to the colour of your surroundings. But you will feel bad doing that. You crave to be genuinely you. You crave being respected for who you are. Being yourself doesn't mean that you can be rude to others and get away with it because "I am just being honestly myself." Showing emotions at work is good and even desirable but not in a way that is undermining or disrespectful of others. That's why respecting yourself includes always also respecting others.

The approaches Anna and millions of other people have tried to make them successful and happy are not working. Trying to fit people into a culture is not only making the people smaller but also limiting the potential of the organisation. There is nothing wrong with you. You just need to know your strengths and start using them. You also understand that you cannot be everything. You need people around you with complementary skills.

Connecting with people, using the skills of different personalities, makes us all stronger. As a creative person, you know that you also need beside you the people who complement your features, so create official and unofficial teams around you. You can be the lighthouse showing the way and have the little lifeboats to float around you for creating value together. Everyone can be creative in their own way, but not everyone uses their creativity. Be the one supporting others to show theirs. There will be situations when you won't survive on your own, and there will be times that the lifeboats will need you to show them the way.

The key to what makes the approach I am writing about work is ease. The target is effortlessness.

Be open about your needs and brave to bring your values and skills to the table. The key is to listen to your feelings.[13]

What feels easy and light, is right for you.[14]

What feels heavy, is wrong for you.

What feels effortless for you is your core.

The relieving bit is that even if you spent years and years changing jobs and feeling a bit wrong everywhere you go, this can be fixed. I have guided many coachees and clients through this journey towards finding their core, towards finding what their true self is and using that in everyday and working life in a way that brings results. I am on the same journey myself.

I know you will have times when you just feel off. There will be times when you feel that no one is really seeing you or understanding you, but you have support. I am walking you through the path based on a lot of experience.

I have worked in many fields in many countries, and I have come across these people. People like you. I have had my battles too, my share of feeling wrong and different, but what brought me comfort and support was realising the power of ease and creating a tribe of people who believe in me and the power of creativity around me.

There will be a day when you do not feel wrong, but instead you find peace in being you. You will feel very confident in yourself, bringing great value to your community.

I feel very passionate about helping people like you. I want to make the world a better place and, to do that, we need to acknowledge the value of different skills. People-centred creativity will both make organisations thrive and the world a better place. Empowering people is powerful, and you can be the torchbearer on this path.

When you become aware of your power, you will notice more and more what you have to give in your surroundings – at home, in your community and at work. You can make magic happen in your everyday life. With ease.

I have a dream to bring diversity into leadership teams and boards. There should not only be people who are made in the same mould. Instead, I would like to see more innovation and creativity in our workplaces, and for these skills to be valued appropriately. I also want to see leadership teams and boards actually becoming collaborative, with people working together towards a common target, using their complementary skills, personalities and experiences. That's why I want to crack the cast of both people and organisations so they can become something more by working together in the future. You will be part of this revolution. Together we are creating a community that drives this change into the business world. I know I can count on you. We are together on this journey of creative power.

CHAPTER 2

MAKING MAGIC HAPPEN IN EVERYDAY LIFE

"…You can hide in a box
You can take center stage
You can go where you wanna go
But the person that you always
take along the way
Is the real you that you wanna show
Always be yourself
But if you can be a unicorn
Always be a unicorn…"

"ALWAYS BE A UNICORN"
BY [15]HELEN ELISE AUSTIN

THE CONTRADICTORY POWER OF CREATIVITY

Maybe you have changed jobs many times.

Did you feel like you were a great fit in the beginning and then you noticed that they didn't want you to do what you were hired to do?

Well, that happened to me too. Many times. I have had many jobs. When I was young, I was praised for my creativity and phenomenal communication and people skills. People got excited and I got things done. I was creating things and connecting people, but when a manager I deeply admired told me, while passing me in the corridor, "I hate blondes", it was a confusing moment.

I still don't know why she said that. It left me confused and disappointed. Later on, I understood that I may have been seen as a threat, even though I didn't realise how I could have been one. People with a lot of creative energy tend to be both admired and feared. We need to have a lot of courage to be who we are. In this Chapter, I will tell you my growth story to becoming a creative leader. Maybe you can relate to it and learn something from my path of trials, errors and successes. You can also feel free to choose to go ahead to dig deeper into the Chapters introducing you to the CREATE model.

LEARNING TO LEAD

I had a massive leap in my career when I was headhunted to become the HR Director of a hotel chain in the Baltics and St. Petersburg. I was then working with the manager who said she hated blondes, and she had not given me a salary raise in several years. By changing jobs, I ended up tripling my net income.

As a sociologist, I had found it amusing that economics students thought they would be in a leadership position five years after their graduation. I did not believe that would happen to me. That wasn't the jargon among sociology students in Finland. But four and a half years after my graduation I found myself in the leadership team of a hotel chain living in the embassy area of Riga, Latvia. It wasn't the first time I had moved abroad, I had been an exchange student in Berlin, but this was definitely a huge leap for me. It was such a crazy opportunity that I couldn't say no. Even if it was as scary as it was exciting.

In the role, pretty much everything was new to me. I had been in HR for four years but in a specialist role. It was my first time in a managerial or a leadership role, my first time in an international role, my first time in the hotel and restaurant sector, my first time leading a team with employees in four new countries, and the first time I was working in English, to mention a few "firsts" on that occasion. Having been a "good girl" and a good student I had thought that a leader needed to know everything. Now I realised that no one knows everything. If you have enough brains and communication skills, and if you are capable of figuring out where to get more information, you will manage. And I did. Looking back, what helped me manage to do it was my creativity.

However, even though I had been praised for my exceptional communication skills before, I ended up at a breakfast table at the hotel with "the big boys", the two-metre-tall men of the leadership team who thought I had communicated badly. They could not specify when and how. After investigating the case a bit, it had been when someone wanted to hide something that they had not done, so instead they made a huge point of a request I had made to hide something else that was undone. That started off a spiral of undefined feedback. It made me realise that in a leadership role it is not enough to communicate well. If someone has their agenda, they are likely to use any excuse they can to make you look bad. In a leadership role, you will always be a target for criticism, no matter what you do.

The job was a very interesting possibility, which I am still grateful for. I learned a lot and we managed to develop a lot of practices and processes together with the team. My boss, the CEO, had recruited me saying that he didn't believe in personality tests. Instead, he looked at the position of my sneakers. I guess I placed my trainers well. I had the capability and bravery to jump. Even if it made me freaking scared.

I became pregnant and moved back to Helsinki and, during my maternity leave, the company was sold. Looking back, I had been hired to get the organisation into selling shape. They didn't need double leadership and I needed to find something else to do. At the same time, I was relieved that I didn't need to decide whether to move back to Latvia with a small child. Instead, I could stay in my home country close to the grandparents of my child.

The person who had recommended me to the headhunter for the HR Director role was Katariina Ahonen, who had been a recruiter at Stockmann while I worked there during my university studies. I often worked as a sales clerk at their department store during the summer and winter holidays and during campaigns whilst I was studying at the University of Helsinki. I had made such a great impression on Katariina as the young and energetic part-time salesperson that she later recommended me to an international HR leadership team role. She had met me later too but the foundation for the trust was built then. She believed I could do it and encouraged me to take the chance when I was insecure about whether I could make it.

Now, being back home in Helsinki, Finland, I was pondering what I could do in my new position as a mother of a small boy. I was fearing a leadership role would be too much for me. I even did teacher studies to have more career possibilities that might be suitable.

And I contacted Katariina again. She said: "You don't have to work 24/7 to be in an HR leadership role. Why don't you contact an agency and see what they have to offer you part-time?" I contacted an HR professional agency to map what possibilities they would have for me. I was quickly recruited through the agency to an advertising and design agency to work as their HR three days a week.

WHEN LIFE DIDN'T GO AS PLANNED

I loved the creative environment: it felt like coming home. Very soon after I started in the HR role at the advertising and design agency, I noticed I was pregnant again. That was a dream come true for me as I had feared that I couldn't have any children because of endometriosis. Before the first pregnancy, I had a significant endometriosis operation but, soon after giving birth to my son, the endometriosis was back and I was told that I would need another operation if I still wanted to have children. So, finding out that I was pregnant despite not having another operation was a very happy surprise for me, but it ended up turning my whole life upside down.

The first reaction at work was: "That's great news!" But after a while my boss, the CEO, didn't talk to me anymore. And my childhood love, my husband, told me that he would leave me. Suddenly, I didn't know if I would have my long-term partner beside me when I was giving birth to our second child.

At that point, I started an internal journey to find myself. I had been with my husband since I was 14. We grew up together. It was very scary to have a small child whilst being pregnant with a second, having a new job and my teacher studies and leading a lecture series at the university whilst having the fear that I was soon to be on my own. That was by far the worst time of my life so far. I cried on the way to work every morning and tried to collect myself when I was at the office. I told a friend at work what was going on, except not that I was pregnant because I was still on probation time. He used to ask me: "What's behind that brave smile?" And I would start to cry and he offered to move me to the side in the glass cabinet where I wouldn't be visible to everyone in the open office.

I had my dream job, I was pregnant with my long-awaited daughter, I had a beautiful home with the man I had thought was the love of my life, and then everything crashed. I was devastated. I had wonderful people around me who supported me. I started to practise mindfulness. I focused on the small, good things in life – to be able to go on, bit by bit. I bought an ice cream on my way to work. I enjoyed drops of water on my face when it was raining. I listened to my steps whilst walking. I was focusing on the light.

I decided that the best thing I could give my children was a happy mother. I started to do things that I enjoyed. My husband was still there in my life, but not beside me as a partner. I tried to get things to work, but too much had been said and done for us to have a future together, and I started to create the new me.

A CREATIVE FLOW IN THE NEIGHBOURHOOD

On my second maternity leave, I became a neighbourhood activist. I had been annoyed that my neighbourhood had a worse reputation than it deserved. I wanted to create a bright future for my children. I ended up leading an open network towards colour, collaboration and positive change. When life didn't go as planned, I needed to reposition myself. When I didn't feel supported at home anymore, I tried to find the light somewhere else. For me, it was in creating a community that made the neighbourhood a better place.

Soon after I started my Kannelmäki movement activism, the number of people in the Facebook group grew from 60 to 2,000. I got a huge four-storey-high statue called The Daydream, in all the colours of the rainbow, moved to my neighbourhood, and we launched the theme of Dreaming Big in Kannelmäki. We said: "You are the movement. How do you want to make Kannelmäki an even better place to live, work and visit?" We empowered people to ideate and act and they were proud of it.

All of it ended up with me being nominated for the award of The Most Positive Citizen of Helsinki. I came third in the competition, which was won by a famous comedian, but the nomination was a huge tribute both to me and to altruistic neighbourhood activism. The crisis in my personal life made me strive for a higher purpose and to reach out to the light.

A friend told me: "It is so easy for you when you can just organise events." What made creating feel effortless, despite living in a very challenging life situation, was that I saw opportunities everywhere. I connected with people and made things happen. What I want to show you is how to create magic in your everyday life. It is possible with or without children. It is also possible while you are living through challenging times. It just requires the right attitude.

Organising events has not always been as effortless for me. There were times when I just dreamed of organising amazing events. I used to spend a lot of time fantasising about events that I would organise but I didn't put it into practice.

When I organised the Children's Dream events in Kannelmäki, it was an amazing feeling; everyone wanted to be involved. We had versatile workshops: music, dance and art. We collaborated with local associations, retailers and the City of Helsinki cultural centre in Kannelmäki. And it all went smoothly. People I didn't know came to shake my hand and thank me for creating such a homely atmosphere in my part of town that they didn't want to move away.

Giving people the space to be creative is important and benefits the whole community or organisation, which results in more happiness. The flow I reached in Kannelmäki is what I am trying to get into business organisations too.

When I was back at work after my maternity leave, I decided that I would have to go through with the divorce. At the same time, the agency I was working for offered me a job recruiting in the nuclear field. It felt wrong. So wrong that I felt physically ill about it, but I did it. I felt like I wanted to hide. I was asking myself, "How do I define myself if I do not define myself through work?" In all its wrongness, that job taught me a lot about myself. I realised it was a step on my journey towards something I didn't know yet. I was learning to be more present, in the moment. At the same time, I processed my divorce and found a new partner.

CREATING MAGIC AND CONNECTION IN THE VIOLIN SHOP

With Guy, I gained a violin shop in my life. Guy is a British violin-maker and entrepreneur. He owns a beautiful shop called How Violins, in Helsinki. I didn't know anything about violins except that they were beautiful. Guy wanted to change the culture in the field and created a shop that would be customer friendly and open. Guy also had a divorce process ongoing when we met, and at that time he didn't care about the shop.

However, I showed him the value and beauty of the shop. We started to organise events and concerts in it. After some time, I told Guy that I wanted to set up a gallery there too. He hesitated. He thought it would be confusing for the customers, but when we got the first art up on the walls, he said: "The art belongs here…" I trusted my gut and visual eye. I did it my way.

I gave a platform for passionate people with different skill sets to come together. We organised events with pleasures for all senses: paintings, photos, handicrafts, ceramics, music, dance, pop-up restaurants, pop-up barbershop, pop-up flower shop, pop-up fashion show, violin-making shows, wine and a friendly, welcoming atmosphere. I connected people from different fields, people who had never been to a violin shop or a gallery before, and it was amazing.

This was all done aside from my day job. People asked how that was possible, but it was. When you do it effortlessly, you bring people together by seeing the opportunities and taking them.

I saw the shop's potential and showed Guy how amazingly he had done. It made him want to upgrade and improve the boutique and workshop and, when he was ready, I was ready to roll my sleeves up and support him to do it.

This is the feeling I want to bring to the business world through coaching and creative leadership.

CREATIVE ACHIEVEMENTS, FEELING SMALL AND FINDING THE PASSION

After two years in the nuclear field, I got my next assignment in a big international IT company where I had space for my creativity. I was an HR Business Partner for 600 people in the Business Services globally. I created a big coaching programme, using both internal and external coaches. We explored people's personalities and I showed the value of creativity at work. Together with brilliant people from all over the world, we achieved a lot. It was a very giving and successful project which taught me and the participants a lot and inspired both me and many others taking part in the process to study coaching. The project still remains one of the most inspiring projects I have led. I took on a new role, which wasn't supposed to be started fully before I got my HR tasks handed over to someone else. Instead, I ended up with expectations to drive through two full-time roles at once and it didn't roll. The learning was to not agree on doing two roles at once… When changes were made in the organisation, I didn't have that consultant position anymore in that organisation, and yet another consulting task was started. I had worked seven years in different roles through the agency and I felt that many times I needed to adapt to a role that wasn't me. I had more to give, like so many others, too, who were being put into imaginary boxes. So, when I was contacted by a law firm, I took the gamble. I had been recommended by a colleague from the IT firm. I challenged them when I was interviewed, "If you want to have someone to roll the papers, I am not your person. If you want change, I might be."

I was hired to take HR to the next level. It felt good to be part of the organisation after having worked externally over the last seven years. I created a wonderful team around me. I also did business coaching training and started to coach, both at work and externally with my Fast Creative company.

I have had many wins and bumps during my career. By that point, I could see that my experience helped me solve many challenging situations, including leading an organisation through the time of Covid. The more unsuccessful occasions have been influenced by challenges in my private life, but we will all have challenges. The key to it is how we treat them. Do we let them take us down or do we choose to create magic in our everyday and working lives despite the problems? I have noticed that, especially when there was something unfulfilling in my life elsewhere, I spiced up my days with creative projects on other platforms. But these two do not need to be separate. I also created a lot while loving my job both at work and outside it. I want to bring the creative flow of collaboration into every business.

You can do that too. Children do not hinder that. A bad relationship does not hinder that. Not even a bad organisation culture hinders it (well, it depends on how bad…). You just have to find ways to take small moments in your life to take things forward. Don't get me wrong, I have been in moments when anything extra felt impossible, but many times when there is a will there is a way. I have the passion to change the world. I want to bring creativity into business life and make that a valued asset and wanted skill. I have the passion to help you have an impact in your community, in your surroundings and your organisation. I want to help you shine.

YOU ARE THE CHANGE

You are the change. Sometimes it requires changing jobs or leaving a toxic relationship to have the space to thrive, but you can thrive in your life even without external changes once you know yourself and your strengths; create a team of people with complementary skills around you and you can see the opportunities and make things happen.

I have worked a lot on my self-knowledge. I know my strengths and weaknesses and I am getting better at using those strengths whilst building networks that support my weaker sides or the areas that don't inspire me. It is a lifelong process, and no one is ever ready. I am here, by your side, on your journey. It may feel scary to come out of your comfort zone, but once you focus on your strengths and do not behave like you think you should, new spheres will open up for you. I am coaching people to feel comfortable about being themselves, and leaders to recognise and appreciate the creativity in them.

I have seen the change in people in the organisations and in the creative projects that I have been leading and with my coaching clients. It all starts from self-knowledge and awareness. You do not need to feel wrong anymore. You do not need to change jobs to try to fit in. You can because you love the change and the energy of the new, but that should be out of your choice and not because you would not be good enough.

When I was in the middle of the saddest time of my divorce process, I found a little flowery pink wooden briefcase which says: "Wherever she went, happy bloomed". I bought it as a reminder to believe in myself. I did not feel that then, but I decided to believe in it.

When life doesn't go according to your plans, it might end up becoming something far more interesting than you knew was possible.

Join me on a joyride of creative leadership.

CHAPTER 3

CRACKING THE MYTHS

"I've been reading books of old
The legends and the myths
Achilles and his gold
Hercules and his gifts
Spider-Man's control
And Batman with his fists
And clearly, I don't see myself
upon that list."

"SOMETHING JUST LIKE THIS" BY [16]COLDPLAY

My friend thought that doing creative things was easy for me, but it was not possible for her. You might also feel that creating change is not possible for you, but that is not true. A lot of people are held back from bringing the creative spark into their lives because of more or less imaginary obstacles. I want to help you to see that all of this is possible. Ignoring or overcoming the barriers will help you to not only change your life but impact the lives of many others. In this Chapter, I will open up the myths that keep us from advancing into creative leadership.

MYTH 1. THIS IS ONLY POSSIBLE FOR PEOPLE WITH SPECIAL CREATIVE SKILLS, AND I AM NOT CREATIVE

[17]Brené Brown says that "there is no such thing as creative or non-creative people, only people who use their creativity and people who don't."

You might not score highly in creativity and imagination in a personality test like WorkPlace Big Five, Big Five or Enneagram, but you can be creative despite that. When you are curious and operate through your strengths with ease, believing that you can do it, a change is possible.

Start by seeing the possibilities instead of the obstacles and feel the bubbly energy of creativity.

It is in you. It may require some digging to truly feel it and make it real, but it is in you. Some people have read this book thinking that they are not creative and got a new view of their creativity and noticed that they are actually creative, in their way.

MYTH 2. IT REQUIRES A LOT OF MONEY TO CREATE NEW THINGS AND ORGANISE INSPIRING EVENTS AND DO MARKETING FOR THEM

Many of the biggest projects I did had zero budget. The key is to find collaboration partners who are willing to give their expertise or to sponsor or sell their services or products. It is interesting what you can receive by just being brave and asking. **If you can paint a vivid picture of something that is about to take place, many people will want to be involved**. If you have a great cause or purpose for your actions, you will be surprised how easy it is to involve people.

When organising Children's Dream events in my neighbourhood, I got everyone involved that I asked. I even got someone to compose a song for the event just by asking if he would like to do it.

When organising fascinating events in the violin shop gallery, I brought together interesting people to a unique space. I didn't need to pay for food for the event because we had a pop-up restaurant each time, and the pop-up restaurant sold the food there. It brought a special element to the event, but it didn't require any investment on my part. We also brought in a pop-up flower shop, jewellery shop, barbershop, fashion show etc. and all of these elements brought excitement to the events but didn't cost us any money.

At the IT company, we gathered together a network of internal coaches and created a massive coaching programme that had a big impact, also without hiring external coaches. The price was the time put in, but bringing together coaches from Finland, Sweden, the Czech Republic, Latvia and India created a big impact on the organisation. With the leadership teams we also used external coaches.

A lot of marketing can today be done for free on social media platforms. You can also do nice graphics for free on tools like Canva. With these tools it is possible to do marketing for the right target groups, either for free or at a low cost.

When thinking out of the box, a lot can be done either totally without cost or with low cost.

MYTH 3. IT TAKES A LOT OF TIME TO CREATE THINGS, AND I DON'T HAVE THE TIME

A lot of the creative things I have done, either within my official work platform or in my spare time, were done in collaboration with other parties. When everyone brings their expertise to the table, you can share the time used.

When I was involved in the neighbourhood activism, the founder of the network said that he used to say that if you gave a task to a busy man then it got done, but after having worked with me, he says, "Give the task to the mother of small children and it gets done."

I organised events during the nap times of my children. I contacted people when it was suitable for me and wrote a message now and then, sometimes in the evening before going to bed, sometimes first thing in the morning. What needs to be clear, though, is that you do not expect an answer during a weird time. Emails can also be timed to be sent within normal office hours. I do not suggest that you should work night and day. What I am saying is that part of the ease comes from doing your things at times that suit you. Bit by bit. Don't expect it all to be done at once, instead break it down into pieces.

Some time management or structuring tools may be helpful. Some people like an excel spreadsheet, others like Asana or the Kanban board to be on top of things. It is good to know what you have going on and what needs to be taken care of. A structured approach doesn't kill the creativity but gives space and time for it.

MYTH 4. I NEED A BIG NETWORK TO BRING PEOPLE TOGETHER

A big network helps in getting your message out through different channels, but what is most important is curiosity, an open mindset and bravely contacting people.

I have contacted people that I have never met, having only read about them in articles or seen them on the socials, and just reached out to them to bring in their art to my gallery or for other expertise. People are, in general, very taken to being noticed and invited to interesting events. If you present your offering in an interesting way, most people want to hear more about it, and many say yes right away. My perspective is always that it needs to feel light for every party, that it gives more than it takes, and I am vocal about that. It is in general something that speaks to people. They know that I am not there to exploit them, but instead to give them a new experience or a platform for creativity.

MYTH 5. IT CANNOT BE DONE WITH EASE; ANYTHING PROPER REQUIRES HARD WORK

Hard work is relative. You have a lot of expertise in your repertory that has been developed throughout the years. You did not receive your expertise for free but have worked to come to the point where you are. However, being impactful doesn't always require hard work.

You do not need to count the hours you worked, but the impact you made. How you make people feel is what matters.

If you can change how someone feels, it is hugely impactful. If you can change the path an organisation is taking it is impactful. It may be a long journey, but small insights can take people and organisations to new spheres.

That's why coaching is so impactful: any small insight can grow into a huge change in a human being's life.

Start taking the steps and you will notice that you have it all in you. Sometimes I feel with coaching clients that they do not need me; they have it all in them already. Eventually, that is all that I have to do: remind them of their worth.

I started a coaching process with someone very creative and she explained her different fields of work to me in a very understandable way. My first reaction was a fear of failing with her as a coach, as I felt she was already so far along on her self-development journey. However, going further in the first session, I understood that she would benefit from the CREATE model, especially because she had so many elements in place, but she did not see it or feel it herself. Sometimes small things done with ease are very significant and sometimes you can move mountains with ease. With the right attitude.

CHAPTER 4

THE CREATE® FRAMEWORK

"Take that ride
On a magic carpet
We can fly
There'll be nothing like it
Feels so right
Every night
Everytime you're near
I get creative."

"CREATIVE" BY [18]LEON JACKSON

THE BUMPY ROAD TO BECOMING A CREATIVE CONNECTOR AND CATALYST

While writing this book, I came across my notes from the year 2013. At the time I was on my second maternity leave. I had two experiences from leadership roles behind me and was reflecting on whether leadership suited me or not.

In my reflective notes from 2013, the bits of leadership that I thought suited me were: being a driving force, innovation, encouraging and engaging people, delegation, strategic thinking and seeing the big picture, alongside my ability to take responsibility and withstand high pressure. However, I was thinking that loneliness and hardness do not suit me. I was reflecting on whether it would be possible to lead together with people without feeling lonely, and if I could be a leader without being hard.

As a leader, you need to be realistic that shit will hit the fan. You will be in challenging situations and you will need to make difficult decisions that may be right for the company, but they will not always be liked by the individuals. Anyway, it is possible to lead as a human being together with the people. Looking back, I have done that and become the person and leader I wanted to be. It is, of course, a lifelong journey and no one is ever ready.

However, if I had then the knowledge I have now, after a lot of moments of both successes and bumps in my career, I would have felt better about myself. I would have respected my special skill set and would have been able to translate that into business language. I have had my share of trials and errors, and my task is to support you so that your road is less bumpy, and you can find your way of doing things more easily and more quickly than I did.

This Chapter introduces in depth the CREATE model and going forward Chapters 5-10 will offer you a deep dive into each area of the model. I will teach you the model of effortlessly making the transition into using a creative, human-oriented leadership style. Don't worry; you have that in you. My task is to help you to see your value and translate that into action. All of the 5-10 C-R-E-A-T-E Chapters include a lot of tasks as well. You can choose to read chronologically since the Chapters build on each other, and you can also dive deeper into the sections that especially interest you.

The framework I crafted is called CREATE. You will learn what the framework is about, where it comes from, whom it is for and where it can take you. In the Cambridge dictionary, "create" is defined as: "to make something new or invent something".

The CREATE framework can be used as a leadership or coaching tool, but it is not only suitable for those purposes. The speciality of the CREATE way of doing things is that, at the same time as you help someone else, you end up helping yourself. You can use it in any field of life. After all, we humans are a whole being and just slicing an imaginary work profile out of you is artificial. With this model, you will learn to see your career and life from a new angle, seeing that you can find an overall fulfilment in life, even if some areas are not what you would wish them to be. With the help of the CREATE mindset, you can start crafting the life you would like to have.

The traditional leader, that in my experience is or has been the respected norm in business organisations in Europe, is what Bill Joiner calls an "expert" or "achiever" in his study Leadership Agility. We want you to go to the next level by becoming a "catalyst" in your surroundings. You will become the creative connector and catalyst by following the CREATE process.[19]

Bill Joiner's expert is a tactical problem-solver, someone who wants people to follow them because of their authority and expertise. The achiever is more strategic and thinks that they can motivate others by making things challenging through contributing to larger objectives. We want you to become the catalyst who is a visionary with a facilitative orientation. The CREATE tool helps you to articulate an innovative, inspiring vision and to bring together the right people to transform that vision into reality. As a creative catalyst leader, you will empower others and actively facilitate their growth.

When you unleash the CREATE energy and mindset you will be guaranteed to have a lot of fun. And that is infectious. You will get your team to work with you.

Are you ready to join me?

DEFINING THE CREATE ROAD MAP

To become a creative leader you need to take the six steps to creative leadership:

1. **C – Curiosity**

2. **R – Respect yourself and others (will too)**

3. **E – Ease and effortlessness**

4. **A – Attitude and acceptance**

5. **T – Take opportunities**

6. **E – Enable**

According to the CREATE model, the steps above take you to creative leadership. To be honest, these steps don't take you there, but you do. It is all in you, and putting the **attention** on the right things, **accepting** who you are, **appreciating** it and finally taking **action** will lead you towards creativity, as [20]Patricia Ryan Madson would say.

Patricia Ryan Madson also states that today's leaders need to: 1) have the ability to change, 2) have imagination – the ability to let the world expand in many ways, and 3) be comfortable with ambiguity. Being in a state of flux is almost the default today. This means that creative leaders are the greatest asset in these times, and we need to raise our profile in the corporate field. Creative leadership is especially useful during crisis times, when you need to find new ways of doing things whilst having inadequate information.

The first four steps in the formula are internal. The following two are external ones. You need to do your internal exploration with Curiosity, Respect, Ease and Attitude, and as a creative leader, you also use the external capabilities, Taking opportunities and Enabling. However, the steps towards becoming a creative leader are not necessarily taken in chronological order, step by step, linearly. Each individual has a different maturity level within these steps. Many of the blocks are advancing in parallel and the progress can be seen before you are "ready" with all these steps. This is a tool both for the self-development of leaders and for the growth of the people and organisations around us. The progress happens on many layers at the same time. Creativity and innovation are complex, and I am saying that you have it in you.

With this model, I am guiding you to find your own approach to creativity.

It requires internal examination and looking in the mirror. It requires deep self-knowledge to be able to see and take the opportunities and to be the lighthouse enabling others.

THE CREATE® FRAMEWORK

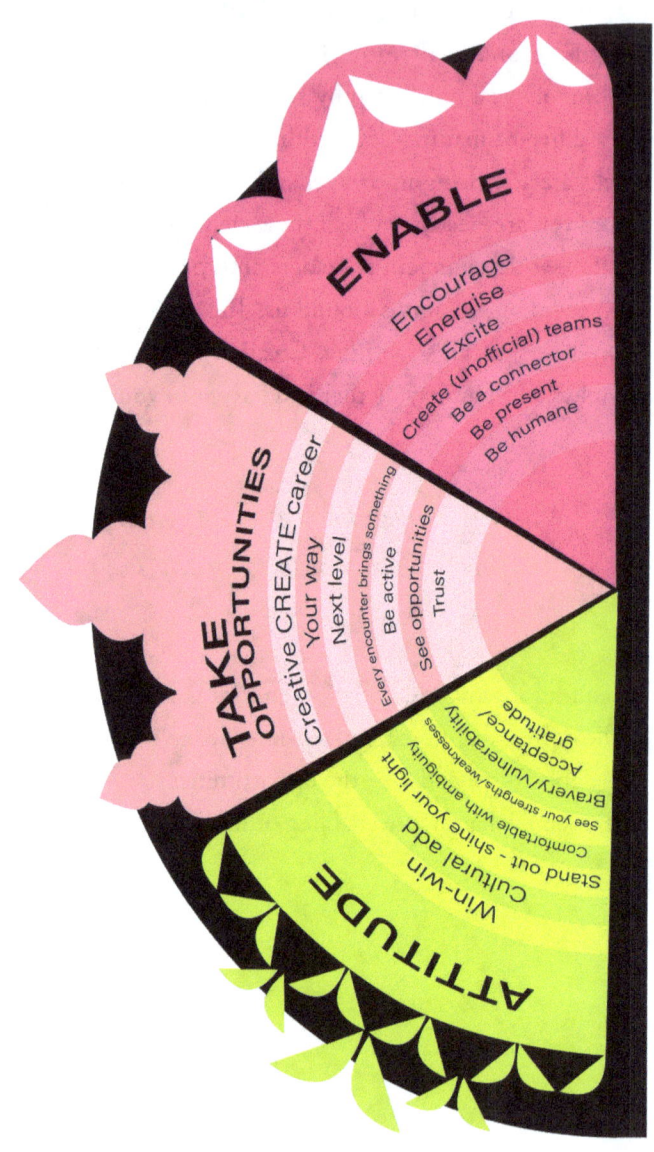

CREATE

JOIN ME STEP BY STEP

Step 1 - C Curiosity is all about belief in wonders. I am going to show you that anything is possible so that you can open up your senses and let the creative energy run through your veins.

Step 2 - R Respect is all about self-knowledge and wanting to develop as a human being. I will help you to find ways to gain better self-knowledge, finding your strengths so that you can find your value.

Step 3 - E Ease (Ea) is all about trusting your gut. I will teach you to listen to your instincts and to trust that you can start doing things more effortlessly.

Step 4 - A Attitude is all about bravery. I will support you to see that you don't have to fit in, because your strength is in seeing things differently. You can shine, be grateful for what is and have the ability to change in uncertain times. Acceptance is the key to this.

Step 5 - T Taking opportunities is all about opening up your eyes to the inspiration of alternative paths. I will tell you about cases that will inspire you to make a change in your (work) surroundings too.

Step 6 - E Enable (En) is all about connecting people and offering them a platform for growth. I will guide you to become the creative leader that you want to be. By bringing people with different skill sets and talents together you can make magic happen.

With the CREATE® spices you can lead creatively in any environment: in a business organisation, a public organisation, association, open network, your neighbourhood, with your friends and family. The red thread throughout your internal and external journey is to trust your intuition.

I will ask you questions throughout the process that will help you to keep on track. The framework includes a lot of material and you do not need to take it all in at once. To simplify it, there is one "Trust your intuition" question following each Chapter that you can ask yourself to keep on track.

HOW CREATE WAS CREATED

I had been planning to write this book for many years, but I never seemed to have the time for it. I have been collecting material and experiences for a couple of decades, and when I started to narrow down my ideas, I realised that all that I had done in my broad and versatile career comes down to creativity and leadership in one way or another.

My path has not been a traditional one, but rather a "portfolio career", as [21]April Rinne would call it, whilst [22]Inkeri Ruuska would describe it as a "career landscape" in her book about multi-skilled people. I would call it a CREATE career.

When graduating from an art high school I thought that I would become something that is traditionally seen as creative, but instead I ended up studying social sciences at Helsinki University, with sociology as my main. For most of my career, I have been working in the private sector, starting first with communication and marketing and ending up with HR and leadership roles. I did not climb the ladder in a traditional vertical manner each time I changed jobs, instead I jumped, at 32, to filling big shoes by leading the human resources of a hotel chain. After that, I had many roles as a consultant, sometimes being in a smaller and more supportive role and sometimes leading and having the main responsibility for my field. I learned to act differently in different roles. I also became a much better subordinate after having been in leadership roles. However, I always found it challenging when forced to fit into limiting expectations or any kind of boxes.

Mostly, I am passionate about work, but when work didn't feel fulfilling, I compensated for that by doing creative things in my private life, in associations, boards and networks. I have been searching for the perfect organisation culture. Although I have worked in many fields internationally, some of the things I did voluntarily gave me the biggest kicks, and I started to explore how to bring that spark and flow to the business world. I want to show you with this book that a career that is not "traditional" is not only OK but desirable.

Seeing and experiencing different things broadens your thinking and raises your capability for creativity.

I mapped the first idea for the CREATE book at the beginning of 2021 in Stephanie Aitken's Female Leader Mastermind. I came across Leila Green and Ali Dewji's writing course for entrepreneurs in Autumn 2021 and found myself participating in it soon after. It was just the thing I needed to fit writing into my tight schedule. It gave me the structure I needed to write down and specify my thoughts that have been crystallised over the years without me finding time to write them. So, whilst this is a new approach in the market, it has been crafted during a longer timeframe with a lot of expertise from leading in different markets and fields internationally, in big organisations, start-ups and open networks.

CURIOSITY AND SELF-KNOWLEDGE AS A BASE FOR CREATIVITY

Children are naturally creative. Adults tend to start acting how they were taught to behave and how they assume will gain them respect. A good example of divergent thinking decreasing when you are growing up is Sir Ken Robinson's classical research from 2011, where he did a paperclip test on 1,500 people. He asked them how many ideas they have on what they can do with paper clips. The most common number of ideas people had on what you could do with a paperclip is 10–15. However, the ones who are very good at it figure out 200 ways. The divergent geniuses are nursery-aged children. Then it starts to rapidly decrease the more education you have about what is possible or what is correct. Divergent thinking is not the same as creativity, but it is an essential element in creativity.

In the same way, as in the paperclip example, new employees often have a lot of fresh ideas, but after a while, you get so used to the organisation that it is difficult to notice what needs to be done and what could be advanced further. Futurist [23]Perttu Pölönen says that future skills are difficult to teach. It is difficult to do a test on bravery or give points on your level of curiosity. Many of the skills you will need in your future working life, as well as being a creative leader, are learned through trial and error and learning through mistakes.

However, [24]Susanna Rahkamo and Pauliina Valpas from Yellow Method have been researching the creative performance capability of the Finnish population with the help of the creative performance index. They say that creativity is a critical working skill that is needed to speed up change in ways of working, utilisation of new technologies and to innovate and develop the working life. The research that is part of the Finnish Work 2030 programme is based on 2630 answers from people in different roles in different fields in Finnish society. The relieving and encouraging finding is that the creative performance is actually increasing with age. The people above 50 years have, in fact, the highest creative capability which correlates strongly with identity, curiosity and drive and, especially, with self-confidence.

It seems that children are very creative and at some point we learn to behave like we think we are expected to. We make ourselves smaller and do not act and operate with our strengths. But when our self-knowledge and self-confidence grow with age we become more self-aware and use more bravely our own kind of strengths, which leads to higher creative performance. Age doesn't bring self-awareness automatically, but if we work on our personality traits and build on our strengths we have all the chances to flourish creatively at an age of 60+. This is also good news for many European countries with an ageing population. We need to believe that we have a lot to give also at a more mature age.

The findings in the Creative Work 2030 report by Rahkamo and Valpas support the framework that I created and present in this book. The CREATE framework touches base with many of the elements that this research highlights, and I will come back to these elements going forward. With the framework, you notice that you can bring the genuine you into the organisation where you work now, and thrive. Change also requires resilience because most people are not ready to move forward as fast as you. To be honest, sometimes there isn't buy-in or capability for change and then it is better for you to move on, but that is out of your own choice and not because you would be wrong. Some organisations just don't have the maturity for the change today's world requires or that would satisfy your progressing passion.

Guest writer

HELENE AURAMO

CEO, Founder of multiple start-ups
(e.g. SLUSH and Prönö)

I believe that businesses that want to exist tomorrow need to be creative. It requires new ways to see the potential futures and act on the most inspiring ones. Anna Moilanen talks about building utopias for companies. I think you can build utopias if you are open-minded and creative.

And all people are creative. It is within us and can also be learnt if one has forgotten how to find the creativity within them.

I have been an entrepreneur for 15 years. I didn't think I was creative before I got into art university. It might sound funny, but I thought I was just a business mind and didn't get too many new ideas. When I started to work with some great artists, creatives and designers, I realised I had several blocks in my head that kept my thoughts and ideas limited and me from being creative.

The creative atmosphere opened my mind. I started to first get some ideas, then more ideas and soon so many ideas that I became anxious. It took me a few months to find a balance. And I think that is how the creative business thinker in me was born. Soon I started my first company with some of my friends.

The easiest and fastest way to be creative is to be curious and open-minded. Read books, talk with different people, write, draw and think.

I try to boost my creativity by meeting different people, being on different advisory boards with other businesses and creative people and by thinking and listening. I try to think every day without any limits. Often, the only limits you have are in your head. Try to locate them and move on.

I encourage you to meet people from different fields and industries – find the thinkers and change-makers. Every day, you can learn something from them, and also about yourself.

THE CREATE APPROACH

What is special about the CREATE approach is that everything is done with ease, effortlessly. My principle with everything I do with individuals and groups is that it needs to feel for all parties like it gives more than it takes.

Creativity thrives in collaboration, and collaboration should always feel like a win-win solution.

Since our logical part is usually analysing heavily and the brain is galloping like a wild horse, you need to trust your gut. If it feels light, it is right for you. If it feels heavy, it is wrong for you. If you are looking to find a logical formula that you do step by step, and each and every one of them is separate from the other, it may confuse you. The different steps in the CREATE approach are partly overlapping, like any personal growth you do in life. Creative things aren't necessarily linear and that is the juiciness of it. To get the most out of this process, you need to get out of your head. Use all of your senses to carry out the new way of being you.

Another reason why this approach works is that it isn't anything external, instead it starts from within. You have it in you. If you are the creative person I am writing for – you know it. If you don't quite feel it yet, there might still be a lot of dormant creative energy in you. If you start to become excited about the thought of not only having creative ideas but putting them into action, this is something for you. If you feel the invisible bubbles starting to spark in your body as a mark of something new approaching, you should read on because this might change your life.

According to the report about creative work by [25]Rahkamo and Valpas, we can identify ourselves as creative people and act creatively. Then we use our creativity to solve problems and ideate new things and to deal with change. For some people creativity is an essential part of how they identify themselves and place themselves in the world. Creating can feel good and bring us a sense of meaningfulness, but it can also feel unpleasant if the end result is unclear. According to the questionnaire, a lot of Finnish people enjoy creating something new, but they may feel that it is challenging to get to a creative mindset and state. This book gives you tools to find your creativity. I can help you see what amazing things you have created, drawing out examples that were maybe too obvious for you or that you didn't see as impactful or meaningful because they were not part of your official career story, or they didn't fit into the cast.

When I heard about Swedish keynote speaker and author [26]Fredrik Hären, who is called the Antony Bourdain of creativity, my first spontaneous thought was: Oh no, someone is already doing what I want to do! And of course, I understand that there are many players in this field, but he sounded so cool that my spontaneous feeling was unease at the idea that someone else had already written about what I wanted to explore. I participated in one of his keynotes in a MySpeaker event. And it was fascinating. Fredrik Hären travels the world to see creative people from different cultures. He researches human creativity and wants to find out how creativity varies in different parts of the world. I realised, though, that his approach is very different to mine. He is a male hero traveller, travelling the world to find new ways to see creativity. I am talking to you. To an ordinary woman or man, a leader and/or a parent, who wants to bring creativity into your own life. I am not researching how other people are creative, I am saying that you are creative. And I will help you to unleash your creativity with the CREATE model. You will get the chance to dig deeper into the model in the coming Chapters. In the table below you see the steps that will become familiar to you throughout your journey.

THE CREATE® FRAMEWORK

Curiosity	Wonder – be in awe	Belief in wonders – anything is possible	Wander – go to places, don't plan everything
Respect yourself and others	Be genuine – transparency	Self-knowledge/self-development	See your special gifts – what is easy for me is not easy for others
Ease and effortlessness	Know your strengths	Mindfulness – listen to your body	Trust your gut
Attitude	Accept what is – gratitude	Bravery – vulnerability	Ability to look at yourself in the mirror – see your strengths, but be honest about the development areas
Take opportunities	Trust	See opportunities everywhere	Be active – don't wait for people and things to come to you
Enable	Be humane	Be present – get excited	Be a connector – connect with people

Imagination	Creative mindset	Be agile – test – redirect – find the way – repeat	Creative energy
Self-value	Humble pride	Respect different people and skills	Together we are more
Just do it – if you fear mistakes a lot of brilliant things get undone	Do things that you burn for – love what you do, and do what you love	Live in the now for the future	Happiness – joy – freedom
Be comfortable with ambiguity	Stand out (don't fit in) – shine your light	Cultural add – not cultural fit	Win-win
Every encounter is a possibility for something previously unseen	Next level – personally, professionally and financially	Your way – not the traditional way	Creative CREATE career
Create (unofficial) teams – bring people together	Excite	Energise	Encourage

WHY THIS APPROACH IS GOOD FOR YOU AS A CREATIVE LEADER

My intention with this book is to support you on your journey towards being visible and respected for whoever you are and whatever you do. Your creative energy needs to be acknowledged. You may have felt that something is off with you, as you didn't seem to fit into organisations, that you were different and strange in the surroundings in which you work and live. Maybe it is because you are different. Maybe you are more observant than the average person and express your thoughts and ideas more often or in different ways than someone else. Maybe you are the black sheep in the family or the odd bird at work. And all of that is OK, just as long as you know your strengths and can also look yourself in the mirror and face your weaknesses. As we all know, any strength is a weakness when overdosed.

You may have already explored your personality style and looked into what benefits other people's skills can bring to the table. Being creative, you probably like having different people around you, knowing that they can complement you and that you are more when working together. If we would focus on changing you, because you feel off or if we would say that everyone else is wrong and you can just act how you please, we would be off the rails with this. That would be treating the symptom and not the root cause. There is nothing wrong with you, but with the help of the CREATE tools, you can start living a much more fulfilling life. After all, once you have unleashed your curiosity, explored your personality style and looked into your attitude and ways of doing things, you are further along on your journey.

The CREATE framework is effective for creative people who are leaders or want to become leaders, seeking to be genuine and to make a change in their surroundings. It also works for those of you who have had a fixed mindset, seeing yourself as not being creative, but are actually called and drawn towards the creative mindset. It doesn't matter if you tried many times and failed. It doesn't matter whether you see yourself as a leader or not. You might not even recognise all the creativity in you. Once you start noting your strengths and seeing your capabilities, you will notice that you have already been leading creatively in many ways. Maybe it was by equipping your children with creative materials. Maybe it was by organising parties for your friends that everyone expected and waited for, as you were so great at bringing together people and creating a warm and exciting atmosphere. It could have been some bigger projects that you did at work, where you really could see out-of-the-ordinary possibilities and solutions, and that ended up being a success even if it felt like dragging a sleigh of stones behind you.

I remember when I told my colleague how I was in awe when my son had, at the age of six, made a perfect three-dimensional living room in a shoebox that I had given him. My colleague looked at me and said: "Maija, your children are probably very creative, but it is not only that. It is the kinds of materials and ideas you give them. I would never in the world have thought of giving my children a shoebox! You are leading them to do the creative things they do."

That was an insight for me. Sometimes the creative things we do are so obvious to us that we do not notice that they are seen as unique by others, things that they would never imagine doing. That's why I remind you to not underestimate yourself. The things that are easy for you are not easy for others. There is a power in the ease. I prefer to not measure things by looking at the hours you have put in, but by examining the outcomes you have achieved and the impacts you have made.

THE TRANSFORMATION OF HOW VIOLINS

I am going to tell you about one transformation case where my CREATE energy and mindset were both useful and successful. I am choosing on purpose a case that is rather personal and that involves both personal development and the support of an entrepreneur who happened to be my partner. It is an illustration of the fact that the CREATE framework can be used in any surroundings at work or in your private life, and you do not need to go through every step every time, instead using the elements that are suitable for the situation at hand. The order does not necessarily need to be C-R-E-A-T-E, but all of the overall steps and letters need to be touched upon. Being mindful of all those elements will bring success even if you do not follow them step by step. Flexibility is the essence of it. Capability to adapt, also while using this framework, is a sign of creativity.

CREATE

INSPIRING AND UPGRADING THE VIOLIN SHOP

I met Guy at a time when we both were divorcing. The big life changes made him consider changing all spheres of his life, and he was planning to sell his violin shop. He was a very good violin-maker and he had worked very hard to become one. He had started to learn how to do it when he was just 19 and had come to the point where he could found his own shop some five years before his divorce. He had built the shop on values of openness and excellent service (A, R). He wanted to change the culture in the field to being more open and respectful towards every customer, whether they were only touching the violin for the first time in the shop or already established as superstars in the field. The shop was beautiful, even though it looked a little bit worn out when we first met. It was rather dirty and the shelves were half empty, but I saw its potential and I loved the space.

I had been studying in an arts high school and the everyday beauty around me had always been something I found very important. One of my best friends was a world-class violinist, but that was my only experience of violin music. Even if the music industry and violin business were very alien to me, I was very curious (C) about them and they fascinated me. I could see the beauty in the handcrafted instruments and ancient handicrafts, also in the philosophy of seeing each customer as a unique musician and human being. I saw the potential (T) the space was carrying. However, Guy was a bit fed up and wanted to get on with his life.

Firstly, I had someone come over to clean the place. Guy had tried to do the cleaning himself and obviously had not had the time to do that properly. When the shop was clean, the customers started to comment that it was beautiful there. (A) Guy started to fill the shelves and, after a while, we started organising events in the shop. (C, R, Ea, A, T) At first it was made up of women's events, with coaching, violin-making and rehairing shows and trials of the different instruments. Then we started to organise concerts in the shop, and people loved the shop. (R) Guy started to see the value of what he had created. He started to respect himself as the violin-maker and business owner he was and saw that he had created something unique.

(Ea, A) Organising the events was very easy and natural for me, but not for Guy. As an introvert, he was perfectly happy to not have too many customers in at once. But together we were good at organising events and, in his space, Guy was very confident and charming. Guy didn't yet see the marketing value of the events for his business. (T) Then I one day said that I would like to put up a gallery in the violin shop. Guy hesitated as he thought he had a concept that already worked well and art on the walls might confuse the customers. He said maybe, and after a while maybe became yes. He said to me, "When I say 'no' it doesn't mean 'no', it means I need some time."

I set up the first art exhibition with an artist friend. When we got the art up on the walls, Guy said, "Wow, the art belongs here." (R, A, En) After that, we started to have continually changing exhibitions because the shop just looked naked without art on the walls. I didn't have experience running a gallery, but I just started to do it. (C, A, Ea, T) I had a keen eye for beauty and a very clear vision of what was suitable in the space we had, respecting the original purpose of the building as a violin shop and workshop. (C, T, En) Around each art exhibition opening, we organised beautiful events where we brought together passionate people with different skill sets. We started to be famous for our beautiful events and more artists wanted to have their art exhibited in the violin shop gallery. (R) Now Guy started to see the value of the art and events for his core business.

He said, one day, (A, T) "I would like to upgrade the space." I had not pushed for it, but when he was ready, I was ready to roll up my sleeves. (C, R, Ea, A, T, En) I found a handmade counter, marble shelves, a Finnish handmade refurbished blue velvet sofa from the 1950s, cushions and new curtains; we remade the showcases and windows and bought old frames that we painted in gold and then we added orchids to the displays. And the shop had transformed into a boutique.

Every customer who came inside took a deep breath when they stepped in… "This is beautiful!" Hotels sent their customers to come and look at the shop on their way to tourist attractions. An Italian customer brought his son, who was studying architecture in Italy, to How Violins "to see what success looks like", as the customer said. Since then, Guy has upgraded the boutique and workshop further, with lighting, designer shelves, handmade ceramics and handblown glasses and many details for the different senses.

Guy had always been ready to take chances (A); he was brave, and he had the ability to change (R), but he had always thought that he was not creative. However, I brought the creative elements and the ease of doing things out of him and into his life.

The changes in the shop did not only transform how the shop looked but also how Guy felt about it; (R, T) he felt pride and he felt that he wanted to succeed, and he was excited. Since then, How Violins has lived through many challenging times. Two years of roadworks in front of the shop were followed by Covid-19 and lockdowns and a crisis in the music industry. Then, when the worst Covid time was over, a façade renovation was started in the building. Small shops have been having hard times during lockdowns, but while the competition was crying for help, (C, R, Ea, A, T, En) we decided to instead support the musicians and created a free TeacherPortal to connect music teachers with new students.

When the newly restored façade was uncovered, the Covid restrictions had started to fade and the world opened up again, Russia started a war in Ukraine, which once again made the customers cautious. Despite challenging times, the How Violins boutique and workshop has been successful in maintaining its customers because of (R, A) the passion and commitment of its owner and by getting new customers to try How Violins thanks to strong word of mouth and by being trustworthy, interesting and inviting. That is thanks to the (R, A) high quality of both instruments and restoration work, and also because it is always enjoyable to pop into the shop for the expertise and a cup of excellent coffee or tea. (C, R, Ea, A, T, En) Guy didn't only get his passion back but found a new, more creative, side to himself. He has worked on the strategy and the marketing, improving the website constantly. He has always been a fighter and hard worker, as well as being multi-talented. Through the new creative elements that brought beauty and prestige to the boutique, he also started to enjoy going to work. Now it is such a beautiful place that he constantly wants to upgrade it and fulfil new ideas.

The CREATE framework and our collaboration was successful for How Violins, but it also gave me a lot of pleasure and satisfaction. (C, R, Ea, A, T, En) I founded a company, started a gallery, gave the opportunity to many female artists to exhibit their art in a unique space and brought together people to experience previously unseen things in unique gatherings.

(C, R, Ea, A, T, En) Collaboration is the essence of creativity. And when you bring people with different skill sets together to create, both individuals and businesses succeed. That's why CREATE is so powerful. It is a win-win way of doing things.

I am delighted to have you with me on this journey. You cannot abandon it now, can you? In the following Chapters, you will hear some examples that can help you to advance ideas about how to use this framework to make a positive impact upon your daily life, your surroundings and the business world.

CHAPTER 5

CURIOSITY

"Tell me, I'm a future seeker

Heat-seeking freak

I want to know now,

I've gotta know now

And no, I know that no,

I shouldn't be so curious

But hell, you got me curious."

"CURIOUS" BY [27]FRANZ FERDINAND

WONDER

"How often do we ponder the depth of the present moment? The one we are in. I mean how often do we really wonder what's within and around us? Afterall, we need to allow ourselves to be moved, to be inspired, to be filled with gratitude for the mystery and the beauty of this universe and of this life…

"So, believe it or not. This story 'Wonder' does remind us how many times we fear the dark only to find that once we enter it there's not something to be scared of. Instead, there is something to be in awe of. Something quite magical.

"When we were kids it was easy: every ladybug was a source of amazement and every flavour of ice cream was a cause for joy. Somehow as we got older we lost touch with that childlike fascination.

"I like to sometimes say that we grew up to know worse."

The story "Wonder" by Chris Advansun is read on the Calm meditation and sleeping app by Matthew McConaughey and his voice sounds like pouring velvet in your ears. I was listening to this story one evening to help me to fall asleep, but these words kept me awake in wonder. I wanted to remember them to pass them on to my children. I got up from bed and wrote them down.

Even if I am naturally very curious and creative, I learned so much of what is right and wrong and what should be done and what shouldn't that I started to question my ideas. I started to listen to the voices of people around me saying, "What are you playing at?", "Do you think you are somehow special?",

"Why do you use your time to help people who don't ask for help from you?", "Focus on your own family and don't distract yourself with other things." There were echoes from people around me who maybe wanted the best for me, but they didn't know what it was. And they also came from people who wanted to put me down.

I started to question myself. I made myself smaller and held back a lot of my ideas. I started to feel wrong and felt that I needed to hide part of myself to be respected and valued at work and at home. I became someone who was not expressing all of my creativity. Luckily, the creativity and the curiosity were characteristics that were so deeply rooted in me that no one managed to pull them out, maybe just slow my growth. But had I been more aware of the value of these features in me, I might have valued them differently.

WHY IS POSITIVE CURIOSITY SO IMPORTANT?

Curiosity is the first step of the CREATE formula. The first of the internal exploration steps on your path towards becoming a creative leader. You need to do your internal exploration with Curiosity, Respect, Ease and Attitude to be ready to step forward towards creative leadership by taking the opportunities and enabling. According to [28]Rahkamo and Valpas, Curiosity is a significant part of our creative potential: it helps us learn new things and to find answers to challenges that we face. [29]Francesca Gino says that "curiosity improves engagement and collaboration". She states also that curious people make better choices, improve their companies' performance and help their companies to adapt to uncertain markets. According to Gino, leaders say that they value employees who question or explore things, but research shows that they largely suppress curiosity out of fear that it will increase risk and undermine efficiency.

A leader can take their team only as far as they are themself willing to go. It requires internal examination and looking at yourself in the mirror; it requires deep self-knowledge to be able to see and take the opportunities and be the lighthouse enabling others.

I am breaking down Curiosity to the areas:

A. Wonder – be in awe

B. Belief in wonders – anything is possible

C. Wander – go to places, don't plan everything

D. Imagination

E. Creative mindset

F. Be agile – test – redirect – find the way – repeat

G. Creative energy

Embracing positive curiosity is living a life in awe. It is being open to the beauty of life. It is noticing the beauty of the shades between the light and the darkness, enjoying raindrops on your face in the summer rain. It is feeling the love you have for your close friends, family and colleagues, or for what you do. It is believing that anything is possible.

Curiosity is about wandering off on different paths, whether you talk about your career or your personal life. Wander in awe and see what you can find.

It requires a lot to keep a childlike imagination. It is easy to adapt and get used to patterns. We seek feelings of safety. We want to feel like we are in control of our life and our work. It is easy to get comfortable with how things are done and to repeat ourselves. Turning imagination into action requires an open and creative mindset.

You need to be able to be agile in your ways of working. In today's world, it is impossible to plan and be fully prepared as something always changes before the planning phase is finished. Living in a flux world you need to be able to adapt to change; hence it is very important to be able to test your ideas and redirect them based on your needs.

When you have all the previous steps in place, you shine, throwing out contagious creative energy.

Picture 2. The Creative Mindset vs. The Stagnated Mindset

Curiosity is the absolute essence of creativity.

Without being in awe of the world and everything that surrounds you, creativity doesn't flow. And yet schools, organisations and adults many times try to kill our curiosity. Here the "adult" means people who have learned to not be creative, adapting to norms and working their way through life, accepting that this is it.

But you know better. You know that seeing the world with fresh eyes is not only more beneficial for you and your business or organisation, but also much more giving and fun. Hence it is critical to keep our childlike imagination alive. To feed it. To nourish it. And to respect that trait in you.

The reason you need to learn the elements of this step first is that curiosity is the key building block of creativity. In the following Chapters we are building on ideas linked to curiosity, and without the curious mind and the open mindset, there will not be creativity or creative leadership.

Guest writer

TUOMAS YLÄ-ANTTILA

Associate Professor of Political Science, University of Helsinki

When I'm taking a walk in a new city and my companion is starting to be ready to go back to the hotel, I'll always want to walk one more block to see what's around the next corner. When I'm at a restaurant in a country where I don't know the language well, I very often get a dish the description of which I can't understand, just to see what it's like. When I was a kid, I'd break my mechanical toys to see what was inside and how they functioned. After having done so long enough, I also started to learn how to put them back together again.

All these are examples of curiosity, a characteristic that feels natural to me, but that I also deliberately cultivate. It makes life more fun. At its best, it is also contagious; hanging out with curious people makes people more curious.

For the curious person, academia is the perfect place to work. One can very often choose a research problem that one is curious about and working towards solving such problems can be very rewarding. Students are often also curious people, and helping them to acquire skills that they need to solve problems that they are interested in is rewarding as well.

In order to succeed, however, the curious person needs to develop strong prioritisation skills. With an abundance of interesting unsolved problems around, unchecked curiosity all too easily leads one to getting involved in too many things. The result can be too much work and doing many things poorly instead of doing fewer things well. But combined with strong prioritisation skills, curiosity can become a superpower that helps not only the curious person but also those around them to do good things, do them well and have fun while at it.

WHY IS IT IMPORTANT FOR ANNA TO EMBRACE HER CURIOSITY?

Let's get back to our avatar, Anna. Anna is a representation of all of us who have started out on the creative journey. She is the archetype of us wanting to express our true creative nature in life and working life. She bubbles with curiosity and is filled with creative energy. Anna knows she has a lot to give, but she keeps feeling like a square peg in a round hole. She is a leader in a big organisation and she keeps questioning herself. Should I even be doing this? Should I be a leader? How should I be as a leader?

Anna doesn't know how she should be as a leader because she has no role models with her qualities. She doesn't want to be the kind of leader she has experienced before. She thinks that no one is like her and so she feels off and wrong. In an organisation where there isn't curiosity, change does not happen. And Anna sees that many things should happen for the well-being of the people and the future success of the organisation. Anna is using a lot of energy to fit into the cast, but she knows there has to be another way.

She has to do things differently, go against the grain, and it needs to start with her embracing her curiosity. Anna doesn't fit into the cast. She knows she is limiting herself and that she needs to be open-minded to get out of the no-no world. It is very important for Anna because she needs the change to happen. She feels bad if she isn't the leader she wants to be. If she is not playing with her strengths she is not as good a leader as she can be. It is also very important for Anna's team that she embraces her strengths, as they are not getting what they could from Anna if she downplays her real strengths.

The consequence for Anna, if she doesn't start to use her curious mind and act based on her values, is that she will keep feeling like she is wrong. She might change jobs, only to find out that the situation and the feeling are both repeated in the new organisation.

THE COST OF LACK OF CURIOSITY

When you open up your ideas to all the possibilities around you, innovations are created. But what happens if a whole company is not curious? It becomes a dinosaur, but the competition is driving or even rocketing past. Kodak invented the prototype digital camera, but didn't use it or react upon it early enough. They weren't curious enough about it and ended up filing for bankruptcy protection in January 2012 while many other companies were thriving through digitalisation efforts.

Curiosity is the building material for everything innovative.

There will never be innovations if a company doesn't have an open and creative mindset, embracing their curiosity. You will just be repeating the old patterns, and the people and the companies with the cool ideas will succeed instead. A brilliant example of a company with a curious mindset has been Tesla, Inc. designing cars that can drive themselves and even moving towards designing rockets. They are doing that at the same time as the automotive industry keeps recruiting employees who mostly only have experience of working with other car companies.

Young people and new people in organisations tend to question the status quo. They have fresh ideas and they express them. However, if they notice that they are not heard and their ideas are not valued, they learn not to bring out their ideas anymore. Or they do but become more and more frustrated because they have not been seen or heard. Have you been there? Did you have a lot of creative ideas, but felt you got stuck? Were you desperately trying to bring out your ideas and got kicked back over and over again?

The primary consequence of not using our curiosity is that it leads to companies that are stagnating; they might succeed today, but they will not tomorrow. What brought us here doesn't take us forward. It will end up with some people staying in their comfort zone whilst others, who feel that they are zombies in their own life, repeat patterns as they fade away personally and professionally. The frustration of the contradiction between your values and what comes through in your working life can even lead to mental health problems and anxiety. There may be pockets of curiosity and creativity in more traditional and stagnated companies, but it is very frustrating for the people who are driving the change in an organisation where most of the colleagues don't see the value of the work they are doing.

Guest writer

SAANA ROSSI

Author, Advisor, Speaker, ex-HR Director

Curiosity has always lived within me and it is one of the biggest reasons why life has always felt like both an endless adventure and a fascinating playground. Curiosity has fuelled my out-of-the-box thinking. It has allowed me to make atypical and creative decisions in both my personal life and my work life, as a leader. At work, my team and I have modified roles and work descriptions according to the employee's wishes. We have created non-standard solutions that both work and inspire at the same time.

Curiosity alone isn't enough to take the required measures. It also requires that you stop to analyse the different alternatives. One has to be open-minded and have the courage and perseverance to try different things and then take the necessary steps. Curiosity is one of the most important (working) life skills. It helps us learn and understand ourselves. With the help of curiosity we're able to deal better with the uncertainties and risks we may find in life.

AS A LEADER, I AM A PARTICLE ACCELERATOR

Just after Christmas some years ago someone contacted me for coaching. She was fed up. She had been hitting her head against the wall for too long in her role in her organisation. She asked me to have the first session as soon as possible in the new year.

My client's ideas and energy were wanted at work, but at the same time she knew she was being narrowed down, made smaller. She was leading big transformations but didn't get a proper mandate or a valid role for making the change. She felt like a caged animal. She was working hard, driving change, but she was also kept under control and not able to bring about real change.

We met for coaching right at the beginning of the year and the woman who had felt caged a little bit too long was bubbling over. She carried quite a lot of anger in her, feeling that she was treated badly, leaving her to smash her head against an imaginary wall time and time again. It required a lot of focus and the use of all my coaching skills to get her to stop and to breathe. I needed to be very fast to be able to slip in my questions to her. As with any coaching, we started by mapping where she stood at that moment and where she wanted to go. She seemed to calm down step by step and feel safer when she started to realise that she wasn't wrong, but her energy and massive drive was causing fear in her manager.

She started to map her strengths as a leader: inspirational, creative, empathetic, driven, curious, strategic. She was a problem-solver with the ability to see the big picture, being adaptive and development oriented. She had the ability to find the questions and the answers, the ability to transform, the ability to change, and the ability to be a change leader… She listed a lot of strengths that would make her a creative and, in many ways, an ideal leader, and yet she kept feeling wrong. It made her angry and cynical. The surroundings she was working in did not see her strengths. Feeling wrong, she couldn't convince the organisation using her best values and strengths, so she kept looking like an angry, caged animal.

I helped her map out where she had come from and where she stood in that moment. She felt that she was, somehow, at the same time both ready to rock and gripped by horror. However, she realised that she was actually ready to roll her sleeves up whilst being in quite a good place because she did not need to make quick decisions.

I asked her to find a metaphor for herself as a leader. She said without doubt: "As a leader, I am a particle accelerator." The engineering inspired metaphor was for her as much of a joke as reality. She really felt that way. She felt she was there to make the particles collide in a way that would make new things happen. Having a name for her leadership style, and having mapped her strengths, she was ready to explore how and where she could use her strengths.

We were mapping her choices of potential paths. She realised that a lot needed to change in her organisation to make her feel that she could make the impact she desired. She understood that she wanted to be in a place where things are done bravely in a new way in an industry that is transforming and where big change happens.

I helped her see the creativity in herself and how that may make others feel. I helped her see her strengths and vocalise them. Her power was unique and that made some people scared, as it often does. When she understood her strengths and started to respect them, she saw that the others might not just be nasty but actually be scared of her power. She understood that she needed to either move to another organisation or help her colleagues to see her with new eyes.

We continued during other coaching sessions to explore the possibilities, and it helped her a great deal to see what kind of organisations would be the right one for her. Eventually, she changed jobs and, when she did so, her previous organisation saw the value in her and wanted her back.

She started to feel that her values were important and she didn't feel wrong the same way anymore. She also understood better how her power could make others feel. Having been very annoyed with people trying to narrow her down, she ended up eventually getting the role that she wanted in the original organisation. She had liked a lot about the firm, but it had started to feel like a too-small zoo for her as she wasn't able to drive the change she wanted. She was finally able to bring her passion in and get a bigger role and make a bigger impact. Sometimes it requires changing jobs to be able to do what you need to do. And sometimes it requires that you leave for your value to be seen. My client needed to have a sideways jump outside the organisation to be seen and valued for who she was, but it was sweet to be called back. She got what she wanted eventually.

It was a huge win for her that her value was seen as soon as she left. There are so many organisations where creativity isn't valued, despite beautiful words in strategies and value promises. A constantly curious mind causes fear in people who like their status quo and feel safe as things are now. In the beginning, people are in awe, but then the fear that something will change starts to arise. When people realise that this might potentially influence their status, or the status quo of the organisation, then fear can become a problem.

How can you overcome that? We will look into that in Chapter 10: Enable.

CURIOSITY

HOW TO BE CURIOUS

I described earlier how curiosity decreases the older children get, as they learn what should and what shouldn't be done. However, curiosity is the base for creativity.

Shoe designer [30]Minna Parikka says that her famous shoes with rabbit ears have a symbolism that is familiar from Alice in Wonderland: follow the rabbit to new adventures – these shoes can take you anywhere. Curiosity requires a childlike imagination. Imagine that you are wearing shoes that can take you anywhere. During the writing process of the CREATE book I bought myself Minna Parikka's glittery rabbit-eared sneakers. They make me feel that I am wandering interesting paths – like a promise of something yet unseen and unexperienced.

The curiosity starts with wonder, belief in the wonders around us and the need for wandering. Open up your eyes and see the world with new eyes (that may require you to put down your smartphone, unless you use only the camera to memorise your observations). Let your shoes take you into new places and see your most familiar surroundings and those closest around you with new eyes. It requires some playfulness, but if the thought of playfulness feels uncomfortable to you, just think of it as observing your surroundings with a scientific mind – be endlessly curious.

You will find tasks in each of the following Chapters that will help you on your path. (You can also download the CREATE workbook at: www.fastcreative.ninja/workbook/).

Intuition will help you through this path. Intuition researcher [31]Asta Raami says that intuition is the basis of thinking. Intuition is used daily by us all, even if it is mostly unconscious. Different scientific disciplines describe intuition differently. According to Raami, intelligent intuition is the basis of common understanding and the core of creative action and innovation. Intuition is not the opposite of knowledge. Most intuitive decisions are based on knowledge and experience. As Raami says, intuition is not a gift given at birth, it is something you can develop further with experience and knowledge. Intuition is your friend on your journey to become a creative leader.

Trust your intuition question

Curiosity: What are the creative things in my life that I do not see?

Gift yourself

When you find new things in your surroundings, you start having ideas. To remember your insights and build on them further it is important to write or draw notes.

Get yourself a notebook that looks and feels good and a pen that feels nice to write with. This notebook will accompany you on your journey towards creative leadership.

TASK

1.0   What kind of notebook will serve my purposes and look and feel good to have with me on my journey?

When I worked in the IT field in a paperless office, I tried for some time to not have any other working tools than my laptop. However, being a very visual person, I needed to get back to my paper notebook habit. To feel good about work, I need to have a beautiful notebook to write in, accompanied by a good pen.

Writing in a traditional notebook will also make you more approachable in meetings, or in a coaching session, because you will not be hiding behind a laptop or other screens. When I wrote my master's thesis I made notes in eleven similar, very pretty, small notebooks, and I wrote with a black pen that was sliding smoothly on the paper. When I started to write my book about creative leadership, I bought myself a notebook with a lilac suede cover, and it feels good in my hands. It also has the small bullet journal dots that I prefer in a notebook. Lilac was my colour of choice because that is the colour of creativity. Before I am releasing the book the lilac notebook is already full of notes and thoughts. Alongside the lilac suede notebook with bullet journal dots I have two notebooks in different sizes with high-quality white paper to draw on. And I have moved to write with gel pens because they are tidy to write with, and it can be rubbered off if I need to. I also have a selection of colourful, high-quality Indian ink pens for my book project. I have other notebooks for other purposes and they all look and feel good.

These are what I need to make notes, but further needs can differ based on the use I have for it. For example, the notebook shouldn't be too heavy to carry around on any occasion because the book is going to be your memory and friend wherever you go, recording whatever you observe, so it needs to be something that gives you pleasure to carry around. Someone might feel this is silly, but opening up your curiosity and creativity requires opening up your senses. This is a very simple exercise of feeling and noticing your senses. Are you ready to go further on your journey towards creative leadership?

When you have your notebook in use, you can use it in many ways. You can have it as a journal on your journey towards leading the creativity of yourself and others. Open your mind and curiosity and imagine what kind of leader you will become.

There are exercises to complete at the end of each of the following CREATE Chapters. Take out your notebook and finest pen and start journaling and answering the questions in this book.

CURIOSITY

| 1.1 | Letter to self: Write a letter to yourself to be read a year from now. |

| 1.1.1 | Where will I be, physically and mentally, on my path towards becoming a creative leader? |

| 1.1.2 | How will I feel? |

| 1.1.3 | What will people think of me? |

| 1.1.4 | How will I thank myself for taking myself this far? |

Remember to thank yourself for having taken yourself so far internally and externally. The length of the path might not be measured in the kilometres you travelled but rather in the impact you made upon your own life, with your family and friends, community and work. You may as well have travelled or moved far from where you are now. The primary target is to make the internal change that will make you a creative leader.

Trust yourself

You will know what is good for you. You will feel what is right and you will get more tools for that when we go further on into this book.

1.2 Be agile in your way of working

Be ready to try things without planning them too much. If you test out ideas and you find that they don't take you in the right direction, re-direct, adjust and move on. You may need to repeat the process. It is not a bad thing. In today's flux world, where everything is insecure and you need to adjust to changes repeatedly, it is important to be able to be comfortable with ambiguity. If you like change you are more likely to succeed and thrive in today's world.

1.2.1 What project or task could I start in an agile way without planning it all through before kick-starting, instead learning and redirecting on the journey?

Challenge yourself

As a creative leader, you need creative energy. I will now describe to you an exercise where you can define where you are on your path towards becoming a creative leader. The point of this exercise is to help you to see where you stand now and where you want to get to.

1.3 Be curious about yourself: who am I?

CURIOSITY

1.3.1 My strengths as a creative leader (write a list of your strengths, as many as come spontaneously to your mind).

1.3.2 Where do I come from? (My home of origin, what I studied, where I lived, what I like…)

1.3.3 Where am I now? (How do you see your development phase as a creative leader?)

1.3.4 Write yourself a metaphor

This describes what kind of creative leader you want to be in the future.

As a creative leader, I am like… (example: a particle accelerator, a unicorn, a rhino, a pool table, a tower block, the sea, the sun, a rainbow, the Statue of Liberty…). Do you notice how the different choices give a different vibe or energy to the image of what kind of leader you are?

1.3.5 Be curious about the future. Where am I going? (What would be the dream target for you?)

> 1.3.6　　Be curious and aware of your needs. What do I want? What do I want to be, have, feel? Remember the different senses.

You probably noticed that this was the exact same exercise that I did with my coachee. She saw herself as a leader, being a particle accelerator. What is the metaphor that you would use to describe yourself? If you want to get deeper into it, it is good to go through the exercise together with a professional coach, but doing this exercise on your own helps you to also move forward on your journey. Good luck on your path… and I'll see you when you are going through the Chapter about respecting yourself and others.

THE KEY TAKEAWAYS OF CHAPTER 5: CURIOSITY

In this Chapter you have learned:

- Curiosity is the key for building your creativity.
- Children are naturally curious. Try to find a childlike imagination.
- Curiosity requires an open and creative mindset.
- Creative energy requires the use of all of your senses.
- The primary consequence of not using your curiosity is that it leads to you not developing and companies that stagnate. They might succeed today, but they will not tomorrow.

CHAPTER 6

RESPECT YOURSELF AND OTHERS (WILL TOO)

*"I used to bite my tongue and hold my breath
Scared to rock the boat
and make a mess
So I sat quietly, agreed politely
I guess that I forgot I had a cho"ice
I let you push me past
the breaking point
I stood for nothing,
so I fell for everything…
…. and you're gonna hear me roar…*

*Now I'm floatin' like a butterfly
Stinging like a bee, I earned my stripes
I went from zero, to my own hero."*

"ROAR" BY [32]KATY PERRY

TRYING TO FIT IN

I have worked in many organisations and in many different fields. I love the feeling of something new. It excites me. I get a kick out of figuring out new things. I have very sensitive tentacles. I sense feelings, traits and ongoing battles in organisations. I love to envision where the organisation should be going based on the facts and feelings that I have learned by observing, interviewing and feeling out organisations.

I see the need for change and I want to be the force for that change. I am the person who brings in something that others don't usually think about. At the same time, I can be a chameleon fitting into different organisations and cultures. It is smooth for me to find my way into a new organisation. I used to forget my strengths and go with people's assumptions and prejudices when I was younger. When I was young, newly graduated and working in the retail business as a sociologist among economists, I forgot that I was good at maths when I was perceived to be a goofy humanist. I should have proudly kept my human-centred worldview and, at the same time, showed my capability for business thinking.

I have many times felt that I wanted to run away. After the excitement of the beginning, I start to feel that I am being revealed. I worry that someone will realise that I don't have it all figured out. But come on, who has it all figured out? No one does! It is the imposter syndrome sneaking in. So, even if I am a brave walker of my own path, I have many times tried to fit in. I have many times made myself smaller so that I would not be too much. I have tried to be less bright and shiny so that I would not make anyone jealous. I have forgotten my strengths to be what I feel is expected of me or to be respected. I felt smaller, forgetting that I am also good at those things that I am not assumed to be good at because of my education, sex, upbringing, or whatever it might be.

Guest writer

STEPHANIE AITKEN

Women's Leadership Coach and Trainer

One of the biggest blocks I see my clients face is the need to adhere to an idealised version of how they think they should be at work. This is constructed from what we believe others expect of us, what we will be rewarded for or what is appropriate for someone in our position. I grappled with this myself early in my career when I was working as a lawyer.

The compulsion to conform can feel very real, particularly when it is reinforced by the culture of the organisation, but it only serves to stifle creativity in the long run. It makes us sanitise our personality, hide behind masks, withhold our opinions, second guess ourselves and more. Instead of respecting ourselves, we betray ourselves in a thousand tiny ways. And we deny others the opportunity to truly benefit from our greatest talents and contributions.

Overcoming the gravitational pull of fitting into the mould takes effort and courage but it is always worth it. I believe it is only when we are truly authentic and own our value, that we really stand out and make our biggest impact as a leader.

HOW TO CREATE MUTUAL RESPECT

One coachee that I worked with had a background of working decades in surroundings where a certain rather stiff and traditional appearance and behaviour were seen as respected. She had adapted to that and kept her private life away from work. However, what she missed most was having a genuine connection with her colleagues. And what she felt most inspiring was to create new things and innovate, even if the field she worked in was not seen as especially innovative but rather traditionalist.

When we started to discuss how she could bring the people closer by starting to open up herself, she had big insights. She started to spark a different, more inviting energy. She noticed that she couldn't expect different behaviour from others if she didn't open up herself. Having adapted to a certain format for such a long time, the change does not happen overnight. But the awareness takes you massively further. At that point, she had tried to fit the format she thought was respected in her role. But that didn't feel right. She noticed that, by changing the energy sent out, she could attract a different presence back, meaning that she developed a closer level of communication with her team. She was looking to gain more respect from her colleagues and realised that it could come through being more genuinely herself at work. Learning to know yourself and your personality, whilst reflecting it towards the different personalities in your surroundings, means that a new world can open up in front of you.

We all have those moments of trying to blend in to be respected. We have a natural tendency to try to fit in. That is biology. That is the survival game. But we are not here to survive. We are here to thrive, and getting to know your strengths and exploring yourself will make you much stronger. You will also need to learn to vocalise your strengths and translate them to a language that others can understand too. If you respect yourself, it will shine through each cell of you. It will be seen in how you carry yourself and it will influence your inner speech. If you respect yourself, others will too.

As a young HR director of a hotel chain, and in my first leadership role, I didn't know what I should look like as a director. Later, knowing myself and my strengths better, I didn't care anymore how I looked. I could just be me.

Respecting yourself involves also respecting others because, knowing yourself, you will also know that you will need people around you who complement your skills. Together we are more. Creativity in organisations is not a heroic myth. It is all about doing things together. [33]Elsbach, Brown-Saracino and Flynn are saying, that "we all know that creative collaboration typically yields better solutions than lone-genius efforts." They address that by taking the time to understand how your colleagues' identities affect their perceptions and actions, and then behaving respectfully towards them, you reveal your own gifts as a collaborator and professional. According to them, the best way to build mutual respect is by spending more time asking the right questions rather than presenting your ideas. That can also be called coaching leadership which is a part of creative leadership.

Guest writer

HILKKA-MAIJA KATAJISTO

Partner Workplace Nordic, HR Director

"Oh, but that's how everybody must feel/think about that!" is something I hear quite often when I work as a coach for individual leaders and team members. It seems to me that most people know with their intellect and from their experience that people are different, but still there is this tendency to think that "normal" is the same for everybody. If we let that misconception prevail, we lose the opportunity to really understand and value ourselves and others. The fact is that our personality traits, which are partly inherited and partly formed by the environmental factors, impact our natural reactions, feelings and comfort zones.

The well-researched and established Big Five model of personality helps us to identify and describe the personality differences, and the WorkPlace Big Five model helps us to uncover meaning from those differences in a work setting. Understanding our own unique combination of personality traits and the many ways that other people can be different is simply crucial for valuing ourselves as we are and other people as they are. Our personality traits are not to be developed but to be respected. What that respect means is that we need to be open to ourselves and to others about what the things are that we find hard and what are the behaviours that we find easy or even comforting. Time and time again I have witnessed how creativity thrives in work environments that are psychologically safe, i.e. where the members of that work community can, without fear, be open about their views and strengths or weaknesses in a given situation. That is the path to creativity that goes beyond one individual's creativity, and it makes us truly become more together.

WHAT IS THE STEP "RESPECT YOURSELF AND OTHERS (WILL TOO)" ABOUT?

This CREATE step (R) is all about self-knowledge and awareness of your own strengths and other people's strengths too. Creativity starts with curiosity, but unless you have a good level of self-awareness you will not know how to turn curiosity into real, impactful actions. The research about creative performance by [34]Rahkamo and Valpas, that I have mentioned previously, states that self-confidence is an essential part of creative capability. In this Chapter, we are building on what we covered in the previous step and exploring how increased self-awareness and self-confidence support your creativity. According to the above mentioned research, mature people have better creative performance capability precisely because they have a better self-confidence than many younger people. It is not, though, a direct correlation that you would have better self-awareness the older you are. It requires the will to look in the mirror and the desire to develop yourself further. With these following tools you get much further with your self-development process.

I am breaking down the second step "Respect yourself and others" into:

A. Be genuine and transparent

B. Value self-knowledge and self-development

C. See your gifts – what is easy for you is not easy for others

D. Value yourself

E. Maintain your humble pride

F. Respect different skills and people

G. Together we are more.

RESPECT YOURSELF AND OTHERS (WILL TOO)

Knowing yourself starts with being brave enough to be genuinely you. It is not an excuse for being a prick. "I am just being myself; hence I can be rude to others…" No, it doesn't mean that bad behaviour is acceptable. But a lot of us hide a big part of ourselves, as we feel that a certain kind of behaviour or way of working is what is accepted and respected.

Learning to know yourself requires self-development and exploring. The ones who have done the most self-exploring know that it is a constant journey and that you are never ready. When you know your strengths, I encourage you to see your gifts. Realising that what is easy for you is not easy for others is an important insight. It helps you to see that something you do with ease can be very valuable, even if it feels light to you. We will explore this more in the next CREATE step (Ease).

All of this will bring you a growing self-value and humble pride. You become humble because the more you know yourself and your strengths, the more you also know your development areas, and this is also linked to being genuine. If you are open as a leader also about your weaknesses, it will make you vulnerable but also more respected. There might be cultural differences here. I noticed working in the Baltics, for example, that modesty wasn't as respected in Latvia as it is in Finland. However, a leader who truly knows themself and embraces that will get more respect than someone who is trying to hide it all behind a hard shell. If you are also open about your weaker sides and vocalise how the team can support you, it means that you cannot be "revealed" by someone else – after all, you have already been open about everything yourself. It all starts with you respecting yourself and others will too.

A leader who knows themself well also knows that they need a team around them to reach the best possible results.

Together we are more.

WHY IS THE RESPECT STEP SO IMPORTANT FOR ANNA?

We are returning to our avatar, Anna, again. Her frustration around feeling wrong, as she does not have real role models for her creative leadership style, is tangible. When Anna gets a chance for further self-exploration, together with the people around her, she starts to see that she has different strengths to the others. They are different but not less valuable. She still needs to work on herself to know her values so well that she can translate that into a language that will have buy-in with her very different colleagues.

It is a huge insight for Anna when she realises that she has gifts that are challenging for others but easy for her. She doesn't need to feel like she is not doing "real" work if she does things she enjoys so much that they feel straightforward and pleasurable. They are part of her super talents that she loves doing so much that it feels easy and light. She finally gets a humble pride in what she is doing best as she is doing it her way.

Anna has always known that the result is best if she has people with different skills around her. She starts to vocalise that more and her team become more and more satisfied because they feel a sense of importance and meaning in what they do. Each individual in the team has an important role and, in harmonious collaboration, the magic starts to happen.

THE COST OF NOT RESPECTING YOURSELF AND OTHERS

Anna can continue feeling wrong and off. She can continue to feel that her way of doing is not right and she can try to work and behave like she assumes she is respected. However, will she get good, let alone great, results? How will her team feel if she doesn't use her skills, instead becoming a lame version of herself as she tries to fit into a cast that is not hers?

We have a lot of leaders who try to be like they think they should be to get respect. They grow a thick armour on top of their skin. They act as if they are hard and nothing can touch them. Mostly, the people who seem the most confident and tough are the people who hide a very hurt child inside themselves.

A hard leader can get a certain kind of respect that can actually be fear. Do people in fear perform at their best? Is it a sustainable solution to tire out your colleagues by keeping them anxious and concerned?

It requires a lot from a leader to reveal themselves to the world as the human beings they really are. In disarming themselves they become vulnerable, and they lay open to criticism of themselves as a person, rather than the armoured soldier they had been playing. However, organisations can thrive only when the leaders are open to being themselves. Psychological safety is built by the leaders. As mentioned before, the leader can take the organisation only as far as they have travelled themselves.

The primary consequence of not showing up as yourself is that it is both emotionally and physically draining to play a role that is not yours. The costs of hiding yourself and your best values are both personal and organisational. Both you and your organisation lose if you try to be someone you are not and if you do not play to your strengths.

WOULD YOU HAVE GUESSED THAT A JUKEBOX WAS THE BUSINESS CARD OF AN ACCOUNTANCY COMPANY?

I have worked with big groups of finance people, engineers or lawyers as their HR. Any group where there are a lot of people in the same profession creates unofficial norms and beliefs on expected behaviour. Working with the finance people, I was constantly noticing that they were talking about themselves as stereotypes of finance people. I challenged them and said: "I don't believe you. You are human beings with different motivators and skills. You are not a stereotype of what a finance professional should look like."

I had the pleasure to have Kay Daniels walk beside me as my "accountability buddy" in the beginning of writing this book. I met Kay through the Authority course for entrepreneur writers. Kay was very excited about my book, but from time to time a bit bored or anxious about her own. She kept saying that finance is so boring. But oh boy did she use her creative mindset when she founded her accounting company.

When she founded her accounting company in 2006 Kay wanted to do things a different way. She wanted the clients to feel supported and she wanted to brand her company differently to the many dry, male-run organisations that you would fear to enter. Kay recruited women to her company and asked each and every one what they wanted to have in the office. Someone wanted to have a neon sign on the wall, someone else wanted to have a palm tree, another employee wanted to have comfortable chairs and Kay's own dream was to have a jukebox. All of the ideas were fulfilled.

The accounting office ended up with bright pink walls, a neon sign on the wall and the heart of the office space was the jukebox. Kay asked every new client what their favourite song was and when they would come to the office for accounting advice their favourite song would play on the jukebox when they entered the office. I was in awe hearing this. Kay had created a very welcoming space for people who feel uncomfortable with accounting and would prefer not to do it. Would you like to enter this space? I would for sure! Kay was running and growing her accounting business for more than ten years, but as it became bigger, she used most of her time running the business and she realised her real passion was to help the clients face to face. Today she does business consulting where she can be in personal contact with the clients and support them to fulfil their dreams.

This shows that not all finance people are made in the same mould. Many people would have so much more to give if they would use their real strengths instead of the ones they assume they should have because they work in a certain profession, or come from a certain upbringing or surroundings. Use your imagination! Do what feels right for you. The circumstances might not originally look like they would enable new ways of doing things, but you would be surprised how much is possible when you just do it.

NOW I KNOW THEY ARE NOT ANNOYING BUT DIFFERENT

When I started to work in a law firm, I wanted to bring self-development more broadly into our ways of working. I had done that in other fields, such as in IT, but in the law field personality profiles seemed to still be a rather new field of exploration. In passion jobs, such as being a lawyer, you can easily burn yourself out wanting to excel. We wanted to give the lawyers as well as our other employees tools for self-leadership, managing their use of energy by knowing themselves better. It was especially eye-opening for people who were not familiar with their personality and who had not looked into how their behaviour might look from someone else's perspective.

We used the WorkPlace Big Five personality profiles to map the different personality styles. Big Five is the most researched personality tool used globally and it shows up to four billion different personality variations. It is exploring five different personality traits that are seen as the most important traits in human beings, and all of them are visualised on a scale from 0 to 100.

We started with self-leadership training and continued the journey by offering each new employee the possibility to have their WPB5 profile. The focus was first on building self-knowledge and self-awareness to support people to see what their natural way of doing things was: what gives and takes energy and helps people to realise how they could be perceived by others. A leader told me, "Now I understand that they are not annoying but different." It was an important insight that annoying became different, and it opened up paths for better collaboration. We started to do team sessions to increase not only their self-awareness but also their knowledge of their teams. Managers started to use their knowledge of their personalities in one-to-one conversations.

Knowing your personality style and the personality style of others better offers a huge benefit, not only in internal communication but also with the clients. Alongside the WorkPlace Big Five Profile™ workshops, we had deep courses on negotiations using the Enneagram tool as a self-awareness base in negotiations. Enneagram has also been used in several leadership development programmes I initiated in different organisations where I have been working.

It all starts from knowing one's strengths and development areas, understanding that any strength is a weakness used in overdose. Seeing the value of different skills and people you become a better colleague, leader and collaborative partner. You cannot be a great leader before you learn to respect different personalities.

The focus on respecting different personalities and skills becomes an integral part of an organisation's culture. As always in these kinds of changes, we are never ready and it requires continuous work. It has, anyway, brought a lot of insights, both for individuals and the teams.

Guest writer

HELI BACKMAN

Organisational Energy Consultant, Executive and Leadership Coach, Co-Founder and Podcast Host

I use Enneagram in my work as an executive and team coach and a trainer-consultant. Enneagram is a framework for self-development and growth. In its core there are nine different personality styles. Enneagram works well for people who want to better understand themselves and their impact on others.

In my work, I see how people become more effective, creative and considerate when their self-awareness grows with the help of Enneagram. In addition, when their self-awareness grows, the same happens to social-awareness. They realise that different things motivate others and that people do have very different needs, for example in team work. Leadership approaches also vary depending on the leader's personality style. Some leaders value big impact and accountability: people doing what they say they would. Some embrace more visionary leadership and a positive atmosphere. For some, connecting with people comes naturally whereas others put almost all their focus and energy on being efficient or acting in a correct manner. There is no best leadership or personality style. The real difference comes from the level of self-awareness and emotional maturity.

I see in my work that such leaders and influencers who have put their self-development as a priority stand out in a good way. They do not just perform well but they bring out the best in others. They inspire others and their way of being acts as a lighthouse for others to follow. They make others feel both safe and brave. Self-development work is not just for you, it also adds value for the people around you. When people feel safe and brave, creativity blossoms!

HOW TO RESPECT YOURSELF AND OTHERS (WILL TOO)

How do you learn to respect yourself and others? It starts with being genuinely you. To get there requires a whole lot of self-exploration, self-development, self-knowledge and self-leadership. Even if you are already far on your self-awareness journey, you can always learn more. Being aware of how you are perceived by others helps you to navigate on your journey. However, acceptance is a huge help.

Trust your intuition question

Respect yourself: What is easy for me that is not easy for others?

Gift yourself

Accept yourself. Accepting yourself doesn't mean that you can act however you want. The better you know yourself the deeper understanding you have of your developmental needs. Leaders tend to be their own worst critics. We demand a lot from ourselves and feel that we could always do better, do more, and do it more efficiently. Many times we also see flaws in our appearance or behaviour: we see ourselves as being too heavy, having too skinny legs, too small breasts, too big teeth, being too clumsy or whatever you can imagine. If we choose to see the flaws in ourselves instead of our charisma, shine or likeability, we are focusing on the wrong things.

Everyone has their own kind of value, which is a combination of your appearance, your values, your skills and your experiences. You are a combination of many things and not just unattached bits. A dog can be adorable, but if you look at only certain bits of it, like its teeth or claws or a drooling mouth, it is not especially pleasant. And it for sure is more pleasant if it is well trained and well behaved. Isn't it much more fun to get home to a dog if it is happily waving its tail to you than if it barks and growls at you? And you see your doggy as the most beautiful and lovable creature in the world. You do not look at its drooling mouth and dislike it because of it. Why would you be so hard on yourself that you condemn yourself for some detail in yourself that you are not satisfied with?

Focusing on details and flaws will influence your feelings about yourself a lot. Ageing or changes caused by illness or accidents can also influence how you feel about yourself, as the mirror shows you something that is not what you are used to seeing as you. It can be very difficult to adapt to your new self, especially if the changes are more rapid. How you feel about yourself shines through to people, either as insecurity or positive self-esteem. [35]Paula Kilpinen had a Keynote speech about one and a half months after a big accident. She had been asked whether she was sure if she wanted to do it anyway after having hit her head badly and sustaining some visual damage to her face. She asked: "What would it tell about me if I talk about it being ok to be imperfect as a leader but would not dare to step up on the stage after an accident? What would it tell to my children, who may struggle with skin problems in their teens, if I could not show up with some scars on my face?"

Everyone who has tried to accept themselves with their flaws knows that it is easier said than done. But try to see yourself with the eyes of someone who loves you. If you feel good in your skin, it will radiate out as someone who knows what they are doing. As a real professional, you will give a good impression in different situations when you can accept who you are and work with those cards you were dealt. You can sell your ideas better, you will convince people around you, and you will end up feeling happier too. Paula, for sure, won the audience with her bravery of imperfection.

The best gift you can give yourself is self-acceptance. That will make you a better leader too.

"Because we can feel belonging only if we have the courage to share our most authentic selves with people, our sense of belonging can never be greater than our self-acceptance" as [36]Brené Brown puts it in her book *Atlas of the Heart*.

TASK

2.0   What do I like about myself? What am I satisfied with? Write or draw in your notebook.

Trust yourself

Imposter syndrome is very common among leaders. You feel that you are not enough and fear that someone will catch you out for not knowing it all and not being on top of it all. You may feel that you might not even be suited to being a leader.

The bigger the role, the bigger the imposter syndrome can feel. One thing that I learned in my first leadership role is that no one knows everything. Not even the person you admire most and who looks like she is on top of everything.

It takes a lot of energy to try to look like you have it all under control all the time, because you don't. No one does. When you realise that no one has it all under control and dare to be genuinely you, expressing also your development areas, you can finally be proud of yourself. That is the humble pride you carry in you. It is humble because the pride involves also the thought that you need to evolve further every day and that you couldn't do it all without accepting help from others.

> 2.1 Draw your life timeline for you from your birth until today.

The CREATE workbook shows you one way of drawing your timeline. Ideate what your timeline looks like.

> 2.1.1 What are my "normal" keypoints, such as birth, start of school and jobs? Highlight them on the timeline.

> 2.1.2 What are the highlights of my life? Highlight them on the timeline with another colour. They can be anything from learning to ride a bike to

> getting into arts school, getting your first leadership role or becoming a parent.

2.1.3 Look at your life timeline from a creativity perspective. Ask yourself: what creative things have I done so far during my life? What could be seen as creative that I maybe did not even consider to be creative before?

Did you organise a big seminar? Do you make handmade Easter decorations each year with your children? Do you love cooking and are great at creating something tasty from what you found in the fridge? Are you great at organising parties? Did you manage to push through a complex project at work which required collaboration with different parties and communication to the employees? Are you great at envisaging strategic changes in your business? Start to see the creative in you. It is in there. You may not have realised how creative you actually are.

Challenge yourself

Explore who you are. Get a deeper understanding of yourself and also of how you are perceived by others. You may have done different personality tests, like MBIT, Disc, Enneagram or Big Five, and all of these tools help you to understand yourself better through self-evaluation. With 360-degree tools, you also get a view of how you are perceived by your colleagues.

If you want to explore further, you can have a personality test done for you. To deepen self-awareness with regard to your leadership development, I have found that WorkPlace Big Five and Enneagram are very useful tools. Remember that, even if your personality test wouldn't describe you as naturally creative, you still have it in you. It just takes a different form in different people. Someone I coached had, according to the WPB5 tool, very low levels of imagination, but he was constantly renewing his business and rethinking ways of doing things. The different test results are most useful when worked through together with a professional coach, and therefore I will not get deeper into personality tests at this point.

You can explore your personality on your own and in collaboration with other people by becoming aware of your behaviour. Are you someone who always wants to say what you think? Are you a good listener, or do you listen just to answer and not to understand the other person's perspective? Do you have a lot of ideas but keep them to yourself only to get annoyed as things are not done in your secret, more effective way? Are you a heavy challenger and perceived as aggressive or difficult to approach? Are you very friendly and bubbly, leaving people questioning whether tasks are getting completed? Try to see yourself through your colleagues' lenses.

What we think when we express ourselves isn't ever received 100 per cent as we intended to share it. Instead, it is perceived and understood through the knowledge, experience and personality of the person hearing us. Communication is hard, and people usually feel that organisations do not have enough or good enough communication.

| 2.2 | What do I look like in my colleagues' eyes? How am I perceived? |

| 2.2.1. | How can I practise my communication skills to build respect? |

| 2.3 | Active listening |

By practising active listening, you can try to really hear what the other person is actually saying. Not only trying to listen but listening to hear. You can practise with your team or with your friends so that you take turns.

| 2.3.1 | First, the other one talks a minute about an agreed subject and you do not say a word. You only listen. A minute feels surprisingly long when you cannot say anything in between. How well did I manage to only listen? Did I have an urge to solve the problem? Did I forget that I was supposed to only listen? Was I good at listening and how did the listening feel? |

> **2.3.2** After you have listened for a minute, you rephrase with your own words what the person has told you and then you change roles. Did I manage to hear what the other person was saying? Did I give an accurate summary of what they were telling me?

> **2.3.3** How am I as a listener naturally?

> **2.3.4** What do I need to focus on to become a more active listener?

In addition to Active listening we also need to practice Empathetic listening where you listen to the other person so that you try to understand them through their perspective. A guide and breakdown of how to do this with additional exercises can be found in the CREATE workbook.

Active and empathetic listening are also features of coaching leadership. A coach doesn't give the answers but helps the coachee to get the insights themselves. It is known to be much more impactful than giving direct answers and suggestions. Coaching leadership is not a pure form of coaching and can be a mixture of mentoring, coaching and guidance. Having the coaching mindset supports respectful communication and develops both people and teams.

When you have explored yourself and tried to see yourself from other people's perspectives, and also practised listening to people from their perspective, you are a long way along the path towards respecting yourself and others. I told you earlier about how one leader had realised after we did the WorkPlace Big Five personality profiles with his team that the others were not annoying but different. Keeping that in mind, many disagreements and misunderstandings can be avoided. If you do not assume what people mean with their words and behaviours, but instead try to understand their ways of acting and reacting, you can be much calmer.

2.4 Time and space: Give yourself time and space.

Keynote speaker and author [37]Camilla Tuominen has said that when she prepares herself for a public speaking event she takes a bike ride or walks. She has her headphones on and speaks the presentation out loud to herself. She has noticed that it gives her the headspace and the state of mind she needs for a great presentation. This way she finds the creative space for a great speech much more effectively than going through slides in front of the computer.

Camilla has also talked a lot in public about her habit of leaving space in her days between activities with the target of never feeling rushed. That sounds wonderful to me, as I have quite a monkey mind and many candles burning at once. I have practised taking my own time, so I take morning swims as often as I can. The day starts better with even a small 5 to 10 minute dip in the morning. I have also noticed that I get headspace in open spaces and high up above the roofs. I love to sit and look at the horizon or wander about by the sea. A boat ride can also work nicely, unless it is stormy. To be by the sea is my favourite place to get headspace, but it works well to also wander about high up on a hill or (even better) a mountain. I also like to go to cafés or bars located above the roofs and have a slow cup of tea or a glass of wine with my notebook.

> 2.4.1   What kind of space helps me think and be creative?

If you do not know yet, this is important to explore. If you feel stuck or in a bad mindset for getting the things done that you have set as a target for yourself, take a break. Move to another room and make yourself a cup of tea and get back to the task at hand. Or go away from the computer on the sofa, to the balcony or outside in the garden, and breathe. Even a small (sometimes only 30 seconds or a couple of minutes long) micro-break can give you the time you need to get back on track and do your thing not only much more efficiently but also more creatively.

> 2.4.2   In a moment of feeling stuck, move to another room or make a cup of tea for yourself. How do I feel after changing space or taking a break?

Instead of being by the computer, take your notebook or drawing pad out and start to write or draw your thoughts. We are talking about mindfulness further in the next Chapter, which is about ease and effortlessness. Giving yourself time and space is at the core of respecting yourself.

> 2.4.3 Write or draw your thoughts on a notepad instead of writing by the computer. Did I notice any difference in thinking when I didn't do it like I would normally do it? Did I get insights or think more deeply if I was drawing on paper instead of focusing on emails and to-do lists at my computer?

Respecting yourself also includes respecting your own energy. As a leader, parent or colleague, it is important to take care of your own energy to be able to give energy to others. Basic things, like sleep, food and exercise, are needed, but it doesn't always require a long run or something very physical to move on with your tasks. Micro-breaks during the day are as important as the bigger breaks. You cannot only live for your holidays and hope that you will recover then. You need to find ways to recover in everyday life. For some that is meditation, others might like to take a run or a hike, whilst someone else could prefer relaxing with animals in nature. You have to find your way to retain and reinforce your energy. In Chapter 7 (Ease and Effortlessness) and Chapter 10 (Enable) we talk more about leading the energy of people and organisations.

Mastering the second step, Respect, you will notice yourself truly respecting different personalities and skills and understanding that you are much more together with people who have complementary gifts. The heading of this Chapter, "Respect yourself and others (will too)", tells you that it is as much about self-respect as respecting others. Once you are confident and respect yourself you will notice that your surroundings do that too. You do not need to agree about everything but being calm and confident builds respect for you. Respecting yourself includes also respecting your time and finding ways to work that work for you.

THE KEY TAKEAWAYS OF CHAPTER 6: RESPECT YOURSELF AND OTHERS (WILL TOO)

In this Chapter you have learned:

- Creativity starts with curiosity, but unless you have a good level of self-awareness, you won't know how to use curiosity in the best possible way to make real, impactful actions.

- Knowing yourself starts with being brave enough to be genuinely you. Learning to know yourself requires self-development and exploration, which in turn will need time and space.

- The more you know yourself and your strengths, the more you also know your development areas. A leader who truly knows themself, and embraces that, will get more respect than someone who is trying to hide it all behind a hard shell.

- A leader who knows themself well also knows that they need a team around them to reach the best possible results.

- Even if you have already travelled far along your self-awareness journey, you can always learn more. Being aware of how you are perceived by others helps you to navigate on your journey.

CHAPTER 7

EASE AND EFFORTLESSNESS

*"...Everybody wants me to be
what they want me to be
I'm not happy when I try to fake it
That's why I'm easy,
I'm easy like Sunday morning
That's why I'm easy,
I'm easy like Sunday morning
I wanna be high, so high
I wanna be free to know the things I
do are right
I wanna be free, just me..."*

"EASY" BY [38]LIONEL RICHIE

THE MIND IS GALLOPING LIKE A WILD HORSE

When I was going through my divorce process, I got a lot of good advice. None of which I could actually take in. I was analysing and creating potential futures in my head and being confused and scared. I wanted to make things work. I made huge efforts to have my relationship last. I wanted to have safety and balance for my children and me. It was a process that lasted many years.

I am a very analytical person, and I have tried to analyse work situations that haven't always made sense. It wasn't until I learned to listen to my body that it became clear to me. The brain feeds the fear. We fear many things with or without rational reasons. I started to study and practise mindfulness. Not very systematically, but I became much more aware of how ideas and thoughts felt in my body. [39]Asta Raami, who has researched intuition, says that when you are facing challenging decisions you need to be able to tolerate change, insecurity and things being undefined. You also need patience to endure the gaps in knowledge that you have. Raami says that you can practise these by observing your physical reactions and becoming aware of them.

I read a book by [40]Dr Dain Heer, *Being You and Changing the World*, where he has a piece of very simple advice: "What feels light for you is right for you. What feels heavy for you is wrong for you." That clicked. It made sense. I started to listen to my body and it became clear: Lightness and ease are what I should be striving towards. Or a better way to say it would be that I should be flowing towards it.

EASE AND EFFORTLESSNESS

When I met my new partner after my divorce, he told me: "Being with you is like flowing water." That is the state I want to create in personal relationships as well as at work. I believe that ease and effortlessness bring results. It is not a bad thing to do something that you love. It will be successful if your work feels like a flowing river.

I respect professionalism and deep knowledge. That is not the opposite of ease. You need a solid basis to be able to do things with ease, but making things work the hard way is not always the best way to succeed. And the key is: what is easy for you is not easy for others.

*Don't underestimate the power of ease.
What is easy for you is not easy for others.*

[41]David H. Maister is asking in his book *True Professionalism*: "Are you having fun yet?" He claims that professional success requires more than talent. He says that it requires drive, initiative, commitment, involvement and, above everything else, enthusiasm. And according to his research, fun and enthusiasm are what professionals lack the most. He says that many people are the victims of their past success and that they do not see that they can choose to work with what they love and with whom they like to work. Maister says that those who really succeed are those who can recapture the magic and excitement that they felt when they were first setting to build

their career. He reminds us that enthusiasm and involvement are the keys, and we do have choice of how we build our career. Doing things with an ease is making it enjoyable and fun. Ease is an element of happiness. Being in a flow and in tune with yourself feels easy. In fact, it is so easy and enjoyable that work might not feel like work.

I have a sign on my kitchen wall which says:

"Don't wait for the perfect moment

Just take it and make it perfect."

It's a great reminder of anything being possible despite sometimes having less fortunate circumstances. Many moments have been made perfect with the right attitude.

WHAT IS THE CREATE STEP EASE ABOUT?

After Respect comes Ease. When you know yourself and your strengths you can start using them in your personal and professional life. Know that ease and effortlessness are not the same as being unprofessional. It is mastering your energy use. This step boils down to happiness and joy and freedom. For creative people, the feeling of freedom is very important.

I am breaking down Ease/effortlessness into:

A. Know your strengths – strive towards effortlessness

B. Mindfulness – listen to your body

C. Trust your intuition (gut) – if it feels light = right; if it feels heavy = wrong[42]

D. Just do it – if you fear mistakes, a lot of brilliant things get undone

E. Do things that you burn for – love what you do and do what you love

F. Live in the now for the future

G. Happiness – joy – freedom.

When you know your strengths, you also recognise what feels effortless for you. It doesn't mean that you wouldn't make an effort. On the contrary, the things you can do with a feeling of lightness are the right things for you. Practising mindfulness teaches you to find ease. If you learn to listen to your body, then you recognise what is right on your path.

[43]Dr Dain Heer introduced me to a very easy tool: listening to and learning to trust my gut. I learned that what feels light for me is right for me, and what feels heavy is wrong for me. This little tool I have shared with many friends and clients.

As much as you need to learn to trust yourself, it is also critical that there is trust in organisations. As [44]Amy Edmondson says, organisations with psychological safety thrive because people dare to speak up and take chances. Organisations where people don't fear mistakes evolve because they are brave enough to express themselves and to also try crazy ideas. That's why I encourage you to just do it. Don't wait for the perfect moment. Take it and make it perfect. If it feels a bit scary to do it, it is probably the right size of challenge for you. Try to not plan the future too much, but live in the now, trusting that everything you do will take you one step closer to something exciting in the future.

It all comes down to freedom. Freedom to be who you are, freedom to use your strengths, and freedom to succeed like you. When you feel free to be you and grasp your true strengths, then you feel a sweet joy and fulfilment.

Guest writer

CAMILLA TUOMINEN

Emotion Trainer, Author of five books about Leading Emotions, Keynote Speaker

Effortlessness and Ease – this is actually a core component of my life. Not only in my professional life, but also in my personal life. When I quit my job ten years ago to become an entrepreneur, I decided that instead of forcing things and trying to fit into tight boxes of how I should be doing things, I would create my own way. I started to trust myself, my knowledge and everything that I have learned over the years, and I allowed them to take a form that would be the most authentic me. This has created a most amazing journey.

I really believe that this is the way everyone should work. Science also confirms that through this "letting go", we can actually find flow. When we are in flow we don't think as much. Steven Kotler speaks about the pre-frontal cortex being deactivated when you are in a flow. When in flow, we are hundreds of times more creative and productive. Through this ease and effortlessness, we can tap into these important future skills and amazing powers that we all have.

WHY ARE EASE AND EFFORTLESSNESS IMPORTANT FOR ANNA?

Our avatar, Anna, emphasises the universality of these experiences. Anna has a lot of talents that she does not even recognise as talents, as they might not be the ones the people around her are striving towards. She has a lot of drive, but her drive doesn't look the same as the drive of her colleagues. One colleague is very target oriented and plans in detail every step to get there. However, another colleague is very detail oriented and feels uneasy if there is anything new on the table; their drive is to dig as deep as possible in a specialised field, and the fulfilment of getting there comes from working as hard as possible.

Anna also works hard. She brings people together to ideate and create and to get to the targets she has mapped out for her team or organisation. What Anna needs to see is that her way might look too light to her colleagues who are used to respecting another kind of approach. Anna knows that she has a lot of insights and experience. Anna is a brilliant connector and has always had many irons in the fire at the same time. She has a talent to get people with her and to sell her ideas in a way that it looks like she didn't make any effort. The truth is that it is one of her core talents and she may not have needed to do much at that moment. She learned to use her intuition intelligently, and the skill was maturing throughout the years by being active, in communication with thousands of people, seeing what impact she could have by being genuine, supportive and collaborative.

If she keeps feeling that her way is the wrong way, even the less respectable way, and tries to approach things in a way that is natural for someone else, then she will just be a shade of both herself and the person she is mimicking. She will suspect herself and imposter syndrome will raise its head.

However, if she understands her greatest values, focuses on listening to her gut and believes that her way is very productive and gives great results, then she will feel amazing. If Anna trusts her gut and feels free to do things that she loves in ways that are natural for her, she will find her happiness.

WHAT IS THE COST OF NOT DOING THINGS WITH EASE?

The consequence of Anna or others not trusting their gut and doing what feels light for them is that life and work will feel hard, and they won´t even know why. For Anna, freedom of choice is very important. Ease boils down to freedom and happiness. If Anna won't do things with a feeling of "flow" then she will feel caged and repressed. She will not be the best version of herself, and her team will have a much worse manager. Therefore, striving towards a flow of ease is beneficial for Anna.

The primary consequence of not doing things with ease is that some things might not be done at all. If you plan everything thoroughly before starting, you might not even get to the implementing phase. As everything is changing constantly around you, and the business world is changing too, it is important to have the flexibility to start things lightly and then redirect along the way. It is about being agile. The other potential consequence of not doing things with ease is that you may not get people to come along with you. If your target is that everything you do should give more than it takes, it is easier to sell your ideas and get people to come along on the journey with you.

Guest writer

RIIKKA PAJUNEN

Coach, Author, Entrepreneur Montevista

The most important thing for me is to listen to my intuition in every little thing I do. I ask myself: will this bring peace, ease and joy, and raise my energies or will it do the opposite? Do I really want to do this and why? These questions led me to my dream job in which I help other people to be genuinely themselves by listening to their intuition. My passion is to create a more truthful and happier (working) life.

It takes a lot of courage to travel through crises and various life situations towards inner peace, which leads to profound trust and ease. After all the struggles, you will notice that the key to happiness is in your own hands in most situations. We all need the struggles to realise where ease and effortlessness in daily life lie. And how do we react when challenges arise? I live listening to my heart, and it tells me what to do, where to go and who to be with. I know that I am always in the right place: either enjoying or growing.

Sometimes my intuition leads me to big changes (moving to the countryside, having a sabbatical year travelling around the world…) and sometimes it guides me towards making better choices in daily life. I always strive toward the truth and it doesn't always please everyone. Healthy boundaries help me to live with ease. One question really shook me: am I ready and open to living a life without any struggles? A life in flow, ease and effortlessness. Or am I too used to a life with adrenaline and problem-solving? Today I can truly say yes, I am ready for ease and peace. There is always an easier way – if you are ready to receive and create it.

DREAMING BIG IN KANNELMÄKI

The day I got back home from the hospital after giving birth to my second child, I read an article in the main Finnish newspaper, Helsingin Sanomat, which said that the Kannelmäki movement had been founded. It was the first positive article that I had seen written about my neighbourhood in a long time.

I had always been annoyed that my neighbourhood had a worse reputation than it deserved. Whenever there was some news about it, it was highlighted with huge letters that something bad had happened. In contrast, if there was something positive, it was featured as a school in Helsinki, for example, but they would never mention where in Helsinki the school was. Unlike many other capital cities in Europe, Helsinki does not have any really "bad areas". There is public housing and privately owned houses next to each other. The balance is not even in different parts of town, but there aren't any slums like in many bigger cities. I wanted my home area to get the reputation I thought it deserved as a good place to live.

Before my daughter was even two months old, I participated in the first Kannelmäki movement meeting with her. The movement was founded by Kimmo Rönkä, who is a professional neighbourhood designer and developer who wanted to give something for free to his neighbourhood. I told Kimmo that I wanted to get the boring grey blockhouses around the train station to be painted with all the colours of the rainbow and he said, "Yes, let's do it! Let's meet the Helsinki city architects." And we did.

I wanted to bring colour and communality to my neighbourhood. I wanted to give my children a good place to live and grow up in. I got a lot of energy from doing something that felt meaningful, both for my children and the community.

I initiated the moving of a huge statue called the Daydream to my neighbourhood. The statue was located in Kallio, another part of Helsinki, and was meant to be a piece of art that rotated in different locations. I contacted the Helsinki Art Museum (HAM) and asked them if it would be possible to move the statue to my part of town. They were so taken by the initiative for an art project coming from a citizen that they started the process to move the statue. The cost of the moving process was some 40,000 euros for the city of Helsinki, and the statue would stay in that location for quite a while.

The Daydream statue, which has the shape of a hot air balloon in all the colours of the rainbow, is for me a symbol of anything being possible.

We organised an opening event for the launching of the statue with the director of HAM Maija Tanninen-Mattila opening it. The artist herself, Oona Tikkaoja, was there too. The location was on Sitratori, outside the Kanneltalo cultural centre of western Helsinki. We planned the programme for the opening together with the Kannelmäki movement people, and we got a famous TV presenter to host the event, a local musician was singing, another local was doing laughter yoga for us in the cultural centre. It was an amazing feeling when we got a cultural centre full of people to laugh at the same time. It was as if the laughter and bubbles filled the house and raised the whole neighbourhood to another level. We had locals baking for the event and the local K-Market entrepreneur offered hot drinks to everyone, as it was in the wintertime. The event was so inspiring that the artist Oona Tikkaoja said that she wanted to collaborate with us further. In fact, the employees of HAM and Kanneltalo were also very taken with it.

We launched a theme of Dreaming Big in Kannelmäki. Soon I started to plan the first Children's Dream event. I was walking around the neighbourhood with my baby stroller, enjoying my maternity leave, and talking to people. I visited shops and asked people if they wanted to participate. I wrote to associations and clubs and asked if they wanted to join the event, all this during the nap times of my children. And everyone wanted to be in. Even the artist Oona Tikkaoja wanted to do the graphics for the event for free and she drove from Turku to Helsinki, some 200km, to have an art workshop for children.

Soon I had the structure for the event ready. We were planning with Kanneltalo cultural centre and the city of Helsinki employees for a big stage to be built on the Sitratori square. For the cultural centre, it was a challenge, as they were for the first time organising a big event with an open network of people and they could not have officially signed contracts. They were very scared that things would not work out. They threatened me and said, "If things are going wrong, we will never work with you again!" The reaction was a surprise to me, but I was sure that it would all go well.

We asked on the Facebook page of the movement what the children wanted to have and created the program on the basis of their dreams. We would have music, arts and play and many different workshops. There would be possibilities to print T-shirts and make badges, make crowns in a crown workshop, a scale model workshop, a dream map workshop, face painting, organised play and dance for children. There would be many different pop-up restaurants held by local businesses and private people. A real estate company wanted to sponsor Fröbelin Palikat, a famous Finnish children's band; the K-Market retailer wanted to sponsor balloons in all the colours of the rainbow with Children's Dream (Lasten Unelma) prints; the local pub owner sponsored soap bubbles. We got Angry Birds toys and clothes from Rovio, and plenty of books from Sanoma, to mention a few sponsors.

The day came and the whole square and Kanneltalo cultural centre bustled with people. We evaluated that there were at least 2,000 participants at once, and much more during the day. People came to shake my hand and thank me for making Kannelmäki such a homely place that they didn't want to move away. It made them feel proud of their neighbourhood and they valued the communal efforts made for them and their children.

I hosted the event with Mikko Piiroinen dressed up as a cat. Mikko had a brilliant idea to let the children sing into the microphone. Some were singing, one child made a somersault, someone else was brave enough to come close to the stage and us. We

EASE AND EFFORTLESSNESS

had so many handouts to give that we could give books or toys or Angry Birds socks or hoodies to everyone who made an effort.

It was an amazing flow of companies, local entrepreneurs and private people who wanted to contribute to the well-being of the local people and our children. People were committed to creating something together for the well-being of the whole community. Another thing that astonished me was that I only had to ask, and Topi Suuronen made a huge effort to make a new tune for the event and the neighbourhood. This is the flow and ease that I try to achieve in any collaboration or work that I do.

Organising the two Children's Dream events have been some of the most inspiring tasks I have completed in my life. And it all boils down to creative leadership and doing things with ease. It was a huge effort, but it felt light. I trusted that everything would go brilliantly. The director of the cultural centre feared it could all go wrong, but when it didn't, we had a colossal moment of communal happiness.

Even today, the Daydream statue is used in lectures and presentations as an example of a piece of art that started to live its own life. And the story continues, as you can see from the cover of my book and the interior in this book that are inspired by the Daydream statue. The CREATE model and other visual expressions of my theory in this book are designed by Oona Tikkaoja, the artist of the Daydream statue.

HOW TO CARRY OUT THINGS WITH EASE AND EFFORTLESSNESS

To be able to go with the flow and do things with ease and effortlessly you need to know your strengths and listen to your inner voice. In the previous CREATE step you learned to respect yourself through self-knowledge and self-value. This step, Ease, guides you into doing things effortlessly. Remember that what is easy for you is not easy for everyone. Something that you learn easily and do with ease can take a lot more time and effort for someone else. Effortlessness and doing things precisely, thoroughly and mastering something to perfection are not mutually exclusive. Mostly, the things that you want to master feel right and light for you and you want to work on it further.

We all have different ways of doing things, and for some people being spontaneous, initiating and taking something into action without further research and exploration is inspiring and brings great results. A different person might research every aspect of the matter, finding different alternatives and deciding to do the thing effortlessly, even if the process itself is different.

I can be spontaneous and a fast decision-maker. I am analytical and I am very fast at mapping different options, seeing the big picture and analysing what could be the right thing for me or an organisation to do. I trust my intuition, or let's say that I have learned to trust my intuition more. It is often such a fast course of action that it might look like something was done lightly for someone who is following the fast phase externally. I do map risks, but I do it by planning potential possibilities and choosing from the possibilities instead of getting stuck with the risks. I have had my fair share of doubts and long processes too, but my natural way is to try to find the opportunities and see what feels light.

Someone I worked with was very much a person who wanted to master things with precision. He was also very analytical, but his approach was very different. He wanted to know things in detail, dig deep and do research into things that he wanted to learn. At the same time, he was a very fast learner and could take in a lot of complex information in a short time. He could create strategies, automate things, draw complex models and he was very fast at building websites. Any hobby or work he started to do he wanted to master to the point of perfection. It might seem like the opposite to doing something with ease, but the things he mastered, he mastered exactly because he felt that the act of doing them was effortless and not stressful. We had a very different approach to things, and also very different and complementary skills, but both of us had found our way towards working with ease and effortlessness and could also collaborate smoothly with each other because of our mutual respect.

Your way of doing things might be similar to one or the other of these approaches or something completely different. However, the point is that you should try to find where your flow lies. Find out what feels effortless for you.

Ease is achieved not by doing things how they are normally done but by thinking and acting outside of the box. It is questioning whether things are done smartly and finding solutions to do them lighter. Ease is being efficient, either by automating everything that can be automated or by having the right people do the right things. A coachee of mine told me that he is efficient because he is so lazy. He wants to find the easiest possible ways to do as much as possible. No one would have called him lazy. It was his way of expressing it. In a team, it is smartest to understand the strengths of each individual and let everyone do as much as possible of what they gain energy from. That way, working will feel light. If you do as much as possible of the things that energise you, then you will gain energy from working instead of having energy sucked out of you. That is, if you also get respect for being who you are and are allowed to bring your strengths to the table. With the following tools, you can become aware of what feels light for you.

Trust your intuition question

Ease and effortlessness: What is the gift I have to give the world which is so light and easy for me that I do not recognise its value?

Gift yourself

Praise yourself for what is effortless for you. Remember that what you do with ease is not easy for everyone. As leaders, we tend to be very critical of ourselves. Tap yourself on the shoulder or gift yourself with something concrete, like your own time, flowers, a new pair of shoes or a nice hotel night or whatever you feel you need and is appropriate. Gift yourself when you notice that you have done something lightly, quickly and with joy and the result is brilliant. What you just did with ease might be something that someone else feels is impossible to do.

I told you earlier in the book about a friend who thought it was so easy for me when I could organise events on my maternity leave – just like that. I was living through a divorce process and had a very heavy time in my life. I chose to do things that lightened me up when it was hard. The same is possible for you. The truth is that organising events and rebranding the neighbourhood was something that brought joy and meaning to me. I am encouraging you to find where your spots of effortlessness are.

TASK

3.0   What have I done lately that was easy and light for me? What have I done that was very successful and gave me plenty of joy and excitement?

3.0.1   How can I gift myself today?

> **3.0.2** How will I gift myself within the next three months?

Trust yourself

I mentioned earlier the simple tool by [45]Dr Dain Heer: "What feels light for you is right for you. What feels heavy for you is wrong for you."

I am adding: what feels effortless for you is your core.

Listen to the signs from your body and trust your gut. We tend to analyse and try to rationalise, but your body is smarter than you know. Have you sometimes had a very uneasy feeling in your stomach when you were in a meeting? Have you felt an awkward atmosphere when you were in a room where there was fighting or disrespectful behaviour? If you noticed the awkward energy probably everyone else did too, but we can practise our senses and be more aware of the nuances. Some people are better at noticing different energies and also better at trusting their feelings. You can be one of them.

> **3.1** When did I notice awkward energy in the room and what was the situation?

> **3.1.1** Did I do something about the situation? Should I have reacted or acted upon the situation?

> **3.2** Start with becoming aware of what is going on around you and how it makes you feel.

Mindfulness is a very powerful tool for life in general, as well as occupational and business life. There are a lot of apps and simple tools available. I have used Calm, Headspace and the Oura meditations. The Oura ring is also a very accurate tool for tracking your sleep and finding your balance. You can use these tools both for peace of mind and better sleep. Sleep also influences how you feel about things. You can look for help from apps, courses or tools, but you can also just start to be aware of what is going on around you.

> **3.2.1** Do I feel that I could benefit from a mindfulness app, tool or course? Which tool will I potentially look into?

One simple tool to use in everyday situations is using the word "Interesting"… to give your brain a pause. If you have a screaming child at home or on the bus, thinking "interesting" gives your lizard brain a bit of time to calm down from the fight or flight mode. Just a little break. Counting to ten can help you to face the child. Your brain takes you spontaneously to the fight or flight mode and the screaming child makes you upset, angry, sad and you just want to quieten the child, but when you breathe… think "interesting"… and potentially count to ten, then you remember that it is a child that needs help and is expressing it the only way a small child can – by crying. The child is not screaming to make your day worse. He is expressing his feelings the only way he knows.

Your lizard brain takes you to the fight or flight mode at work when someone accuses you, misunderstands what you said or interprets you in a way you didn't intend. Fights or disagreements at work can be exhausting. We also have very different ways of reacting to things. One person invites "a good old debate" and another does everything to keep the space harmonious. That is why, in the previous Respect Chapter, we learned about respecting different personalities.

Changing the way of thinking to "interesting, why did he react like that instead of taking it personally?" takes us further. The message is never going through to the receiver the way the sender thought it would or should. Everyone is reading things from the perspective of their own experiences and understanding. Someone misunderstanding you is not your fault or their fault. You might have expressed yourself more clearly but, no matter whose fault it was, they understood it the way they understood it. People do not often hear to understand, they hear to answer. Asking yourself why they interpreted it that way is much more interesting than blaming them or feeling blamed.

| 3.2.2 | What moments do I remember from my life when I would have benefitted from pause – breathe – interesting...? |

| 3.2.3 | How will I start practising it (e.g. at work, with my children, with my parents)? |

EASE AND EFFORTLESSNESS

The warm-hearted football coach Ted Lasso says in the AppleTV+ series: "Be curious, not judgemental". He claims that the ones who didn't succeed in life were, in his experience, judgemental instead of curious. We make so many assumptions every day in our private life and working life instead of saying, "Interesting, what can that mean? Where did that come from? How did that thought evolve?…"

[46]Byron Katie has a very powerful tool in her book *Loving What Is* where she tries to help people to overcome their assumptions and challenges with a few questions. She tells people to ask themselves: "Is this really true? How would I feel if it wasn't true?" Very often we assume things that make us feel bad and it might have been an assumption in the first place. It sets you free to understand that a lot of what you think is really only made up of assumptions. If you are interested, you can read more about that in Byron Katie's book.

> 3.3 Ask yourself in a situation where you assume, e.g. that someone is against you or has been talking rudely or disrespectfully about you at work: Is this really true? How would I feel if it wasn't true?

With these small tips and tricks, you can do things with ease. You are no longer burdened by assumptions and heavy burdens. It is of course easier said than done. We are human beings after all, and our thinking patterns are deeply rooted. But, if you become aware of your thinking patterns and ways of working, then you can listen to and trust your intuition more often. That helps you to move towards things that make you thrive. It is a process and therefore you need to challenge yourself.

Challenge yourself

We all know that it takes time to transform but baby steps can be taken every day. We have explored above some practices that can set us free to do what we love. The next step is to dare to do what we love.

Picture 3. Ikigai

Ikigai is a Japanese concept that means "a reason for being". Ikigai connects a) what you are good at, b) what you love, c) what the world needs, and d) what you can be paid for. What you love doing and are good at is your passion spot. Following your passion is important, but not everything you do needs to be extremely useful. If it is something you enjoy, it can have indirect effects on your work performance or on you as a partner or a parent. What you love and what the world needs is your mission. The examples of the Kannelmäki movement projects could be this for me. What the world needs and what you get paid for are a vocation. What you are good at and get paid for is a profession. In the sweet spot where all of these meet is Ikigai. It is a target that you can strive towards but isn't always reality. Finding your Ikigai is one way of finding your spots of Ease.

> 3.4 What am I good at? What do I love? What does the world need that I can also get paid for? There I will find my ease-spot, my Ikigai. What is that for me?

Finding your fulfilment doesn't necessarily mean that you should quit your job and start knitting or painting for a living. You can have a job that might not bring the level of enjoyment you would want but instead create things that bring you joy in your spare time. You can also create a passion business alongside your day job. People have more and more varied careers that involve many layers and elements. You can lecture at the university; you can have a blog or vlog or write articles; you can be a keynote speaker; you can organise events or run a gallery. Careers do not look nowadays like work once did, from eight till four and then home and stepping vertically on the career ladder year by year. For some people it does, but what brings joy to you?

I do not say that you should be passionate about things in your spare time and then settle for a job that you don't enjoy. I encourage you to strive towards fulfilment in all fields of life. But it is unrealistic to think that you will feel 100 per cent fulfilled in all fields all the time. That's life. But with your creative energy, you can make everything better. You can be the change in your life, surroundings and organisation. You can create your kind of career, a creative CREATE career.

3.4.1 What brings me joy?

3.4.2 What does my CREATE career look like?

You have probably heard too often: you have too many ideas, we tried this already and it didn't work, or something else that is putting you down and hindering you from feeling that you can do the change. But when you just do it, amazing things can happen. If you fear mistakes, a lot of brilliant opportunities will be missed. And what you will regret are the things you didn't do rather than the things that you did. Even if you might sometimes hit a rock and need to fix the boat and start over again.

Psychological safety helps a great deal with empowering you to do things that you fear. Bravery doesn't mean that you don't have fear, but instead that you do things even if it feels scary. And if you wouldn't feel any butterflies in your stomach, it wouldn't be a big enough challenge for you anyway. Dance with your fear. Not all organisations offer the psychological safety for you to do new things or do things differently. However, as much as there can be pockets of creativity in stagnated organisations, there can also be pockets of psychological safety in an organisation that does not encourage creativity and risk-taking. You can be the one creating that with your team. By modelling brave and open-minded behaviour, your team and collaboration partners start to dare more too. [47]Jitske Kramer says that "people shape cultures and cultures shape people." Even if the change of a culture is a long process, you can influence it with your own behaviour.

THE CIRCLE OF INFLUENCE

Picture 4. The Circle of Influence

| 3.5 | Draw your circle of influence in your notebook. |

| 3.5.1 | What can I influence in my personal life? What can I influence partly? And what elements can I not influence? |

| 3.5.2 | What can I influence in my work/career/organisation? What can I influence partly? What are the elements that I cannot influence? |

Focus on what you can influence. If you use energy in things you cannot influence, it feels like dragging a sledge of stones behind you and you will feel frustrated when you cannot improve things. When you focus on what is within your sphere of influence, you can build up more energy to take things forward. It's those sparks of ease that give you the energy to drive through difficult things. The areas you can influence partly require more persistence and resilience, but can turn out to be areas of big changes when your surroundings are ready for it.

With these tools, you are already far along your path towards becoming a creative leader. We will check your attitude in the following Chapter and, after that, we will get to the external steps.

THE KEY TAKEAWAYS OF CHAPTER 7: EASE AND EFFORTLESSNESS

In this Chapter you have learned:

- To trust your gut. What feels light for you is right for you. What feels heavy for you is wrong for you. What feels effortless for you is your core.
- Ease and effortlessness are not the same as being unprofessional. It is mastering your energy use.
- To never underestimate the power of the things that feel easy for you. What is easy for you is not easy for others.
- Not to wait for the perfect moment. Just take it and make it perfect.
- Ease is an element of happiness. Being in a flow and in tune with yourself makes work feel easy, so easy and enjoyable that it might not feel like work. That will make you feel free.

CHAPTER 8

ATTITUDE

"It's you, it's you,
it's you I'm talkin' to
Well, you (it's you) you (it's you), you
I'm talking to now
Why do you look so sad and forsaken
When one door is closed, don't you
know another is open."

"COMING IN FROM THE COLD"
BY [48]BOB MARLEY

ATTITUDE AND ACCEPTANCE

To demonstrate what I mean with the fourth step, and the last of the internal process steps, I will tell you a story of a big loss and show how you can change a challenging event to something that will open up new possibilities. When I got together with my partner, he was living in an old wooden house. It had been his dream to have a house with a garden on four sides, and when he achieved that it made him feel successful.

When we got together, we kept our own homes and lived together, travelling back and forth between two homes for many years. We had both just divorced and didn't want to rush into living in one household too soon. It was also important for Guy to make the house look like his own after his divorce. He put money into renovating it. I had from the beginning the sense that the house might be mouldy and not healthy to live in, but the relationship you have with your home is emotional and Guy didn't want to see that possibility. I let it go for the time being and decided to try to hope that there wouldn't be anything wrong with it. When he later took a loan to renovate the house into good selling shape, I told him, "Please have the condition of the house checked before you put in more money." And he did. And the house was condemned. He was told to move out right away.

He lost hundreds of thousands of euros. He still had the land, but the value of the land was not as much as the mortgage, so he needed to keep paying the mortgage to be able to sell the land. He suddenly had a big mortgage for a black hole. A house he couldn't use. Everything in the house needed to be cleaned or thrown away. We found Guy and his son a rental place as the next step while his son was still on holiday with his mother. We didn't have the energy to sell my house and start that process too during the same hassle. The rental place we found was fresh, spacious and on the top floor of a four-storey building. It had a huge balcony overlooking fields and the sky. Finding a nice flat felt like good luck in the middle of a disaster. We were pretty devastated. We had been travelling quite a lot before, doing small weekend trips and some longer journeys to see family and friends and to explore new places. Now we felt that we would not have the money to travel for a long time.

This moment required creativity. How would it be possible to get above the oppressive feeling? Instead of travelling abroad or planning yet another trip, we made ourselves sushi at home. We put on the kimonos that I had bought for us the Christmas before. We sat down on the balcony and enjoyed our self-made sushi listening to Japanese music and laughing at ourselves under a bright blue sky. The burden felt already a little bit less heavy to carry. Guy accepted the situation and had the strength to overcome something that would have taken down many other people. The skill of creating a small space to escape to in your everyday life became more important than I or anyone else would have expected when Covid-19 would soon hit the fan.

I have to admire my partner for having the strength and courage to carry yet another challenge in life, with style and without self-pity. Before he contacted the building inspector, he had already explored what the worst-case scenario could be, and whether he could take it, and only after he knew he could take the hit, he contacted them. Guy had done his internal process and accepted the result, even if it was heavy to carry.

Instead of crying for help or applying for an addition to his mortgage or additional loans, he decided to upscale his rental business, which he had just started. After a while, the rental business made so much money that he could keep pouring money into the black hole which used to be the home of his dreams. He survived that hit.

We also decided to not live like we were only managing something heavy. Instead, we wanted to enjoy our lives. We didn't want to think that we could not do anything because of the black hole in our lives, so we started to plan new trips. Half a year after the big loss, we made a trip to Portugal to a five-star hotel to celebrate the decade shift. It felt like something a little bit over the top for the situation, but it gave us hope.

We welcomed 2020 on a rooftop pool terrace in Portugal. We were drinking champagne in the clothes that we were supposed to wear for our wedding at the big international love party that we were supposed to organise the following summer. I was wearing a beautiful, deep red Karen Millen nightdress and Guy a tuxedo. It was the first tuxedo he had ever owned. As lovers of delicious food, we started the year with style, having a massive food extravaganza. We decided to believe that everything would be OK. We could never have guessed that soon after that Covid would start to spread all over the world. And, well, the planned wedding party was postponed, as were so many other things too. But the rental business kept growing.

At the end of 2020, with its ups and downs, we rented a beautiful, luxurious Airbnb villa in the Finnish archipelago for a long weekend. Enjoying the outside jacuzzi and the beautiful villa with designer furniture and a sauna with a full glass wall overlooking the sea, we felt again inspired and believed that anything could be possible. In that villa, Guy wrote in his little yellow notebook that in three years he would be rid of the mouldy house problem. That was one and a half years after my partner had lost his house. When we came back home, Guy had received an email from someone saying that they wanted to buy the land. A month later the land was sold and the rest of the mortgage was sorted out, to be paid within three years.

This example is very tangible for many people in Finland, although it doesn't tend to happen in the UK or some other countries. The building structures of the houses are usually different as well as the relationship to mould. In many other countries you would treat the mould somehow but not lose the house without any insurance compensation. In Finland, mould is seen as very unhealthy for you. No insurance would cover it if you found mould in your house. If you sold your house and mould was found there within five years, the new owners could legally have their money back in full. It happens to people regularly, and mould being found is one of the biggest fears of people who own a house. As a British citizen, Guy could not have guessed that this could have happened.

WHAT IS THE CREATE STEP ATTITUDE ABOUT?

Attitude is about accepting the situation and trying to find a solution instead of burying your head in the sand and dwelling in self-pity.

The example above demonstrates something bad that happened and how that was overcome. The right attitude can, of course, be seen in positive situations too. But let's face it, bad things happen and your happiness and success depend very much on how you relate to those moments and incidents. Can you find things to be grateful for even when you carry a heavy burden? Can you see ways to get out of the situation?

We see a lot of very smart, critical thinkers in our business organisations and our surroundings, people who find a lot to criticise, but who do not provide solutions. The right kind of attitude in creative leadership is the solution-oriented attitude that sees possibilities instead of obstacles. [49]Caroline Webb asks in *How to have a good day*: "Why do we prefer to avoid situations where we lack information?" She answers that, one reason is that it makes our brain work especially hard. When forced to assess as many scenarios as possible it takes a lot of energy. Not knowing what's going on makes us more sensitive to negative experiences, and it enhances the sense of

ATTITUDE

threat. And yet sometimes we appear to enjoy uncertainty, as Webb puts it. But according to her, what is striking about the uncertainty that we enjoy, is that it is bounded to specifically defined elements of the situation.

Acceptance of the situation helps you to get forward emotionally and concretely. This step in the CREATE formula is all about having the attitude that you will find solutions. In challenging situations, and life will bring them to all of us, acceptance is the key to moving forward. If you feel that life is just happening to you and everything is unfair, then you will be miserable. However, accepting the situation, finding reasons for gratitude, even in moments of despair, and reaching towards a better tomorrow will take you forward.

I am breaking down Attitude to:

A. Accepting what is – gratitude

B. Bravery – vulnerability

C. Ability to look at yourself in the mirror (see your strengths, but be honest about the development areas)

D. Being comfortable with ambiguity

E. Stand out (don't fit in) – shine your light

F. Being a cultural add (instead of a cultural fit)

G. Win-win.

[50]Brené Brown says that what is common for people who can feel pure joy is practising gratitude. Not only a grateful attitude, but actually systematically practising gratitude. Since my

children were very small I have asked them in the evenings, "what are you grateful for today?" Sometimes the answer has been I don't know, or that I got an ice cream or for PlayStation time. And sometimes it has been something incredibly deep and insightful for a small child. I hope this practice will carry them through challenging times in life.

I have always thought that real bravery is admitting that you need help. Real bravery is showing your vulnerability. Many people build a strong shield on their surface and hide their real, true selves inside. The little child who wants to be acknowledged and loved for who they are. It is not brave to have a bold or aggressive surface hiding the real human being. It is far braver to show up as you. [51]Brené Brown has done a lot of respectable research, books and public talks related to these topics.

A brave human being also dares to look at themself in the mirror, seeing their strengths and weaknesses. Attitude boils down to being brave enough to be comfortable with ambiguity. That is one of the core skills of the leader of today. We live in a world where nothing is permanent except change. If someone has difficulties relating to new situations it will become heavy. The attitude I am talking about is related to being comfortable and even enjoying the change. And knowing that you were not born to fit in but to stand out. You will have the attitude to know that you will always be a cultural add rather than a cultural fit. With the right attitude, you create win-win situations wherever you go.

Attitude is the last one of the internal steps. However, I remind you that these steps are not taken linearly, instead they may overlap with each other. Someone might have a great attitude but not as deep self-knowledge. Someone else is very curious with a lot of bravery but feels that things cannot be done with an ease. We all have our own way of deepening our knowledge and understanding of our own creativity. When you master C-R-E-A Curiosity, Respect, Ease and Attitude, then you are ready to start leading others with Creativity.

Guest writer

RAJKUMAR SABANADESAN

Leadership Consultant, former child soldier

Our attitude is reflected in the way we act in our daily lives. Since our attitude is learned, we can also develop it to be more positive. Even if our innate and acquired qualities are average in some respect, we can achieve great success with a super-positive attitude. According to some studies people are up to 31 per cent more productive when operating in a positive state of mind.

When I was about five years old, my mother told me something, perhaps the most valuable thing ever. She told me, "Son, remember one thing in your life: no matter what happens in your life, there is ALWAYS a good reason why that happened to you", and she continued, "especially if that issue makes you feel terrible at that moment."

This message from my mother is in my blood and I live and breathe accordingly.

Several years ago, a person I love and respect deeply told me, "Raj, your problem is that you don't have problems." As a child, in the war, I had seen and experienced things that no child should see and experience. Later, as a teenager on the battlefield, it was all about attitude. There was suffering, death and destruction all around me, and all I could think of during those hard times was my mother's gift.

Steve Jobs once said, "We can only connect the dots looking back." I believe our attitude will have a great impact on how the dots look and feel when we look back at them.

We can all make the choice as to how we want to relate to the things we can influence and decide or the things we don't have any control over.

As Mahatma Gandhi once said, "Be the change you want to see in the world". I think he talked about the importance of attitude.

When we were born, no one promised us a fair life. It is not about what happened to us, it is about how we choose to experience it.

ATTITUDE

WHY IS THE RIGHT ATTITUDE IMPORTANT FOR ANNA?

You know our avatar, Anna, so well by now that you know that she is struggling between what feels right and genuine for her and what seems to be respected. However, Anna has walked further on her path as a leader and by now she knows that she can show up as herself. Bravely, she has become more herself.

She keeps having moments of doubt. And when she has them, she feels uneasy and not capable, and she ends up performing badly or not up to her level. When Anna makes herself smaller than she is, in order to not annoy the surroundings, she ends up not being the best version of herself.

However, in the moments where she finds the right attitude and accepts the reality and plays with the marks she got in life, she is thriving. She is shining like the North Star and people want to follow her. The difference is like night and day. Anna's team loves her. She has their back. She embraces their skills and personalities and helps them thrive. And all of that makes her shine too.

She loves change, so she isn't as uneasy as most of her colleagues in a world that is constantly changing. During crisis times she feels that her creativity carries her. She knows she has something to give that not everyone has, and she starts to be more and more comfortable about being herself. Anna sees the opportunities and she creates win-win situations wherever she goes.

THE COST OF NOT HAVING THE ATTITUDE

The cost of not having the right kind of attitude is that you shrink. You will feel stuck and end up miserable. How would Guy have felt if he had surrendered to the mouldy house? If he let the loss of his house take a grip of his life. If he thought that because something bad happened to him he couldn't live an enjoyable life anymore, he would live the rest of his life with debt and misery. It was a heavy thing to take on, but finding a solution put him on top of it, instead of the problem being on top of him. Not to mention how Rajkumar would have felt if he was letting the war memories of the past also define his future...

[52]Caroline Webb says that sometimes even though the difficult moment has passed, we are unable to let go of it. We sulk about a person who has wronged us or about the unfairness of the situation. While it is normal and healthy to reflect upon what's going on in our lives, obsessive rumination is not helpful, Webb adds. She advises to reappraise the situation. According to Webb, reappraisal involves exploring alternative explanations for what we observed, acknowledging that it's possible that we do not have the full picture. She advises us to 1) list the true facts, 2) highlight the assumptions you are making, and 3) generate alternative interpretations.

Our avatar, Anna, could let her doubts run through her veins and she could let her somewhat more conservative surroundings define her. However, she chose to go for the win-win. She chose to thrive and shine with her strengths. She started to be brave enough to take the rest of the people with her on her path towards creativity and success.

The primary consequence of not having the attitude and acceptance is that curiosity and innovative ideas don't become reality. You can dream and imagine things, but without accepting the situation and influencing the things you can influence, and having the bravery to act, they remain a dream. The attitude also requires the bravery to take on opportunities, which is something we will be talking more about in the following Chapter.

MAKING MAGIC HAPPEN IN EVERYDAY LIFE

Creativity is not a hero myth. You can make magic happen in your own life. When Covid-19 hit Finland, we first had a spring in a closed country. The people who lived in Helsinki were restricted to a small area around the capital city region. We were not allowed to travel to our cabins, that a lot of Finns have around Finland by the thousands of lakes and by the sea. We never had a total lockdown, so we were allowed to enjoy nature, which we have all over the place in Finland, including the capital city area. The forest areas ended up being crowded and the city centre was like an empty ghost town.

During the summer we could not travel, we could not invite guests over or go to amusement parks and do the things that we would normally do with our children. I was thinking of what kind of experiences I could offer our new family to compensate for the lack of things people would normally do in the summer. Eventually, in autumn, I surprised my family. I had a limousine drive into our garden on a beautiful Friday at 5pm. We had dressed up with the family for the special occasion.

It is not something we would have thought of doing otherwise, and it was super fun! We had champagne with Guy and the children got crisps and coke and everyone enjoyed it. We listened to music, danced and the children were looking out of an open limousine window, waving at people walking on the beach while we were driving past the seaside. After an hour-long ride, we drove back to a local Italian restaurant to have a nice meal. It was only an hour of our life, but the impact was big.

A one-hour limousine ride might seem like a cheap thing for some people, or completely unaffordable to someone else. For us, it was something unique and we enjoyed it. All the events I organised with the Kannelmäki movement I did with zero budget. The events and art gallery openings I have also done with almost no budget. I just created a network of collaborators around me.

Making magic happen in your surrounding doesn't necessarily mean that you have to have a lot of money. It just requires the right kind of attitude. "Believe" as Ted Lasso would say. Anyone can do it with the right attitude. By learning the CREATE steps, you will have all the possibilities to change not only your life but the life of your family, friends and community.

ATTITUDE

You do not have to have especially favourable circumstances, actually quite the opposite.

Crises many times create a need for creativity.

Rajkumar Sabanadesan, who has both experience being a child soldier in Sri Lanka and a refugee in Finland, told me that creative leadership is crisis leadership to him. Creativity takes us through challenging times, especially if we can collaborate and find new ways of supporting people.

Covid, with its restrictions, hit the music and entertainment field like a bull in a china shop. How Violins felt its share of it. We didn't start complaining about how hard it was for us, because the musicians were hit especially hard. We saw potential in how the people who were at home were more likely than ever before to embrace new hobbies. Even if many were laid off and worried, many had a lot of extra time and some had extra money too. At the same time, we wanted to do something to support the musicians. In spring 2020 we launched a free TeacherPortal to connect music teachers and students. A portal that we had planned to launch for a long time but never quite seemed to have the time for. We used the short Easter break in 2020 for building up a platform to support the musicians to get some work. It was a tool that became a saviour for many musicians, and a tool that helped many students find a music teacher.

A man whose amazing creativity, grit and resilience I am not alone in admiring is Henri Alén. Henri is not only a Michelin-Starred Chef but an incredible innovator and creator. He owns five restaurants in Helsinki, and you can only imagine how hard it has been to keep the employees occupied during all the lockdowns and Covid restrictions. A lot of restaurant workers were laid off or fired during that period.

What Henri Alén has done has been incredible. He has collaborated with multiple people and organisations to keep the wheels turning. He gained a contract with a car company to borrow nice cars to start delivering food to people at home. That was also a great marketing opportunity for the car company, as Henri has a huge network of followers. Henri Alén created concepts of half-prepared food to be cooked at home to get a Michelin-Starred experience and to feel like a top chef. When the restaurants were closed due to Covid restrictions, Henri Alén instead collaborated with hotels and served food privately in hotel rooms. He has made tasty children's food and other food products for sale in supermarkets. In addition to that, he also collaborated with other restaurants selling food accompanied with a beer or soft drinks outside in pop-up restaurants during the lockdown. The list of innovative ideas is endless. Henri Alén won a prize for The Strategy Act of the year 2020 for brave, creative and flexible leadership during Covid. He was, to my knowledge, the first-ever chef to win a strategy prize in Finland. In awe of all these efforts, I have also been an active fan, using these newly created services that he invented with his team. So have many others. He made it in a way that all of us customers felt that it made a difference when we chose to use the services of his company. That kept his businesses alive and, hopefully, thriving through very challenging times.

Henri Alén had the attitude in place, but I would say he would tick any box in the CREATE formula. He definitely takes the opportunities, which is the following step in this book.

PRESENCE AND ACCEPTANCE

The time of Covid has been heavy for so many. The first months in spring 2020 were pretty rough for me as they were for many others too, as there was not much information; there was a lot of fear, and I was alone for several weeks with my children. I don't know how much was thanks to the mouldy old house and how much was Covid and needing to be apart, living in two households, but we ended up moving in with my partner in the summer of 2020 after some five years of living in two homes. We found a great home to start our full-on new family life.

It was good to be home. After the first few weeks of trying to find our place, all five of us settled down. I was working remotely most of the time. My life shrank to our living room, where I had my office, even though I had global contacts throughout. The movement became minimal, and I had a lot of physical problems. Eventually, I ended up putting on a lot of weight during a year and a bit. I wasn't the only one. Many others got so-called Covid kilos as well. But it impacted me a great deal. It made me feel like I was getting old and incapable. In fact, when I had my 45th birthday that made me feel that I was sliding towards the scary 50 and towards not having value on the market anymore. That was me, who had always been promoting the capability of a woman at any age. Me, who had always thought that a woman was at her best age on any given year.

I was in deep self-pity for a while, kind of on purpose. I knew it wasn't healthy to have bad self-talk, but I felt that I needed to feel low for a moment. The natural way for me is to reach out to the light but I felt that I needed for once to permit myself to sit in the shadows for a while. Then I started to look for ways to feel better about myself. I needed to see the strength, power and beauty in me through someone else's lens. I wrote to a Facebook group of female entrepreneurs that I wanted to find a photographer who takes empowering photos of women. I got more than 340 comments in two hours. I wasn't alone with my feeling it seemed. I didn't go through all of the suggestions. Shanshan Gong was mentioned in several comments, and I had come across her work already several times before, so I contacted her.

We had a wonderful, fun and powerful full-day photoshoot with Shanshan some weeks after the first call. She really captured it all: my power, my beauty, my vulnerability, my happiness, my sadness… me.

Shanshan told me that she felt our photoshoot had been somehow magical. She said she reached a level with me that doesn't always happen with her clients. I asked what was so magical to her about it, and she answered, "It was the presence. It was the acceptance. It felt like anything is OK and I can take chances and it will all be OK." The acceptance had been tangible, both for the model and the photographer;

hence the result was great, because we both put all of us into it and thought "let's play". We knew we would find new sides when we just let things happen.

That is the beauty of the right attitude and acceptance. Attitude is the last of the internal steps before we get to the external steps. Opportunities are to come.

HOW TO HAVE THE RIGHT ATTITUDE

In the Chapters about Respect and Ease, we explored our core values and what brings us joy. That is a great base for knowing how to act in challenging situations with your best features. The attitude of accepting the situation and finding solutions is the core of the Attitude step.

Accepting what the situation is means, in this Attitude step, that you accept that certain things are happening around you, and so you focus on what you can change within those circumstances to make the best out of it for you and your surroundings.

Trust your intuition question

Attitude: What am I grateful for today?

CREATE

Gift yourself

Give yourself the gift of being genuinely you. It requires bravery, but when you show up as you, you will be the best version of yourself. If you have not already done that, I suggest you watch the amazing TED talk "The Power of Vulnerability" by [53]Brené Brown, available on YouTube, which has (at the time of writing) over 56 million views. Even if you have seen it, I recommend having another round from the perspective of finding the creative leader in you. Dare to be you and live and work using your strengths whilst understanding your weaknesses. When you dare to be you, you see your maturity level and strive towards being the best version of yourself. You also accept that you cannot have it all in you and you are better off when you collaborate, ask for help and create (unofficial) teams around you.

As mentioned before, when I was having moments of self-doubt, and going through a rough time, having rapid changes in my body, I gifted myself a photoshoot session with Shanshan Gong. It was very empowering to see me through someone else's lens. I have also organised many events: women's evenings, parties and many events in my gallery where artist Liisa Rasinkangas painted intuitive portraits of the participants. In the women's events she painted us nude – the ones of us who dared. It was very empowering and freeing to get a representation of yourself from the artist's viewpoint. How you see yourself influences not only how you behave with people close to you, but also how you are perceived as a professional.

Another important gift for myself has been taking the time to write this book. It gave me back my self-confidence and belief in me after a period of self-doubt. It has been a joy to write and I have noticed and remembered how I love writing. I also feel physically better and healthier.

TASK

4.0   How will I gift myself in a way that encourages me to be myself and to build on my strengths?

4.0.1   What are the things in my life that will show me the value of myself? How can I be proud of myself?

Trust yourself

When I was going through my divorce and living through a rough time in my life, I decided that the best thing I could give to my children was a happy mother. We carry a lot of weight and expectations from centuries back with regard to how a mother should be. My mother model was very sacrificial, but I realised that, in order to be able to be a good mother in the circumstances that I was in, I basically needed to put the oxygen mask on myself first. I gave myself the permission to create a different version of motherhood than I had observed and learned. That meant that I would start to do things that I enjoyed and suck in every little drop of enjoyment from them, even though I was living through a painful time in my life. It could be just a few seconds of peace with a teacup in my hand. It could be a dance in the rain whilst my children were napping. It could be an ice cream on my way to work. The focus was on creating a happy me to have energy to give to others.

Since then, I have realised that it applies to many other fields as well: the best thing I could give to my partner, my friends or my employer is a happy me. Working in a big IT company, a very hardworking and work-obsessed female director told me once: "Maija, you have such great energy that you will always have people around you who want to take their share of it. You have to make sure that you have energy for yourself so that you have something to give to others." That was for me very powerful when it came from her, who was also a woman very much dedicated to her work. It felt like she gave me permission to also take care of myself. Sometimes we need an external nudge to give us permission to behave differently than the surroundings, or how we would naturally do. People who are very committed to their work rarely take a proper break for themselves, and modelling sustainable work would be important not only for your own well-being but also for the people around you. How could you give the permission to yourself to do things in a different way than you learned from your family or community?

What are the learned thought patterns in your life that are harmful to you? Did you learn to accept that you were talked over? Did you learn to hide the real you and build a hard surface that requires a lot of energy to maintain? Did you learn that you need to show that you know everything and therefore you are not ready to listen to others? What makes you feel that you need to have the answer to everything? I have had coachees who carried these beliefs. What pattern did you learn from your parents, your grandparents, early teachers or supervisors that might not be productive for you?

Create a definition for yourself that helps you out of that pattern, and then start to follow it.

Examples

- I am worthy to say what I think. The best thing I can give my parents, colleagues and supervisor is my honest opinion.

- The best thing I can give my family, community, colleagues and supervisor is a genuine and vulnerable me. They will see my real strength through me showing up as me.

- The best things I can offer my children, teammates and co-leaders are high-quality questions. By helping the people around me find their own insights, instead of me solving everything for them, I will be more impactful as a parent and as a leader.

What is the thought pattern that you need to establish to be able to create win-win situations in your surroundings?

4.1 My cast cracking definition is...

Trust yourself and rewrite the thought patterns you have into something that is taking you forward. Write a definition that sets you free from ancient roles, myths or family-learned expectations. Write your definition in the beautiful notebook that you gifted yourself earlier or in the CREATE workbook that I crafted for you. Writing things down is very powerful, even if you don't get back to what you have written regularly. Many times, if you get back to something you wrote a year ago, you will notice that you already did that, or started living it, even if you had forgotten about writing that. Don't try to be someone else, instead be active in writing your own story. By being you, you do not need to target being a cultural fit in your organisation, instead you can proudly be a cultural addition.

Challenge yourself

As a creative leader, you will be comfortable with ambiguity. Having the ability to live in a constantly fluctuating world and the capability to deal with ambiguity is a must. When everything is uncertain around you it helps to have simple routines that help you to feel grounded. You can also accept more uncertainty when other parts of your life are in balance and you feel good about yourself.

One tool to finding meaningfulness in your life is to map what is meaningful to you and then funnel down your targets from what you want to achieve in three years to the targets for today.

4.2	What is meaningful for me?
4.2.1	First, write a list of people and things that are important to you.
4.2.2	What do I want to reach within three years?
4.2.3	What do I want to reach within a year?
4.2.4	What do I want to reach within a month?
4.2.5	What are my high priority targets today? Check at the end of each day whether you have reached your daily targets and evaluate how meaningful it felt.

4.2.6　　　Draw five diamonds after each priority task, and fill in or colour them on the basis of how well you completed them. How well did I reach my targets?

4.2.7　　　Draw five hearts after each priority task, and fill in or colour them on the basis of how meaningful your accomplishments of the day have been. How meaningful are my results of today?

You can also utilise the tools drawn for you in the CREATE workbook.

If you write down your main targets daily, then you will notice that you have achieved a lot, even if you haven't done everything that you planned. If your priority task for the day was to be present for your children, that can make it a meaningful day, even if you haven't felt fulfilled and successful at work. Colouring in all the five hearts for that day will make you feel that you did something meaningful, even if you didn't succeed with everything you did.

If your priority task was to lead your matters successfully in the leadership team meeting, the day was a success if you succeeded in that, even if something else was postponed to the following day from your to-do list. This is a very merciful tool that shows you what your priorities are. Having a structure for the day and a list of your priority tasks gives you the patience and resilience to take the ambiguity around you. When you feel focused and calm, then you get the space to create new things and lead people through uncertainty.

4.3 Using your creativity makes you a stronger leader.

Challenge yourself to not fear your own light. You have probably tried many times to make yourself smaller so you would not be too much. For some people, your endlessly creative mind, which sparks out an almost blinding light, is frightening – so you learned to dim your light. You don't have to do that – instead, shine your light.

4.3.1 How do I dare to be openly me with all my strength and creative energy?

Work from the perspective of your strengths, trying to understand your opponents. Strive always towards collaboration, which brings win-win situations. Competition brings win-lose situations, avoidance means both parties lose, accommodation means that you lose and the other party wins. To build creative leadership we target win-win situations. Listen to the other parties. Create together and both parties will shine.

4.4 The Mirror

It is bravery to dare to look at yourself in the mirror and admit your flaws. It is much easier to see development needs in others than yourself. Even if you are so far along your developmental path that you understand the areas you are targeting, it is often very difficult to find the motivation to change the areas that need to be further evolved. You can also compensate for your weaknesses by creating teams around you. To motivate you and challenge you, get pens that you can use to write on a mirror, and write messages to yourself that you see every morning or every time you go to the bathroom. Change the notes regularly so that you won't only pass the text by but instead pay attention to it.

4.4.1	What are the areas in me that I can develop further?
4.4.2	What kind of skills and personalities do I need around me in my team(s)?
4.4.3	What does my bathroom mirror tell me? (Write a message for yourself with pens intended for writing on glass.)

Now you have reflected your internal world already quite a bit. Attitude is the last of the internal steps and, in the following Chapter, we will move towards taking opportunities. Open your eyes to your surroundings and you will start seeing an endless flow of opportunities around you. You are ready to take other people with you on your journey.

THE KEY TAKEAWAYS OF CHAPTER 8: ATTITUDE

In this Chapter you have learned:

▸ Acceptance of the situation helps you to move forward emotionally and concretely.

▸ The right kind of attitude in creative leadership is the solution-oriented attitude, seeing possibilities instead of obstacles.

▸ Real bravery is admitting that you need help. Real bravery is showing your vulnerability.

▸ Attitude boils down to being brave enough to be comfortable with ambiguity.

▸ Accept that certain things are happening around you and focus on what you can change within those circumstances to make the best out of it for you and your surroundings.

CHAPTER 9

TAKE OPPORTUNITIES

"Under the glow of the very bright lights
I turn my face towards the warm night skies
And I am not afraid of a thousand eyes
And there above five hundred smiles
Oh I used to think What wouldn't I give
For a moment like this This moment, this gift!
Now look at me and this opportunity."

"OPPORTUNITY" BY [54]QUVENZHANÉ WALLIS

THE OPPORTUNITY OF MY LIFE

Taking opportunities is the first of the external steps in the CREATE formula. To be a great creative leader you have to fulfil the previous steps: Curiosity, Respect yourself and others (will too), Ease and Attitude.

When I started as HR Director of Reval Hotels at the age of 32 it was an opportunity that I could not miss. Moving to a new country, working for many countries in my first leadership role. Leading an HR team of 12 people in four countries, leading 12 hotels in a new business field together with very experienced leaders; I was definitely not certain of myself, but people who had seen my work in very different roles had seen my curiosity, attitude, bravery, communication skills and natural way of interacting in a way that made them recommend me and encourage me to give it a go.

It scared me a lot, but I knew I would regret it if I said no. I had the Curiosity in place. I also had the Attitude in place. It wasn't an easy task for me, but I was brave enough to just start doing things with Ease. I found the right partners, and I found the network and information that I needed to fulfil my tasks. I hadn't gone as far as I have now within the Respect step. I still had some self-exploration to be done so I could better understand my strengths and value, allowing me to better respect myself as a leader. I also didn't have as much experience as I have now. Thanks to my creativity I did manage in the role, but I was just starting to practise becoming the creative leader that I am today.

However, we all have to start somewhere. Once you recognise your values and strive towards creative leadership, you are already much further. The reality is that everyone must do their own trials and failures to find their own path. I cannot help thinking, though, that if I had seen this kind of formula 14 years ago I might have believed in myself more. I would have seen how much I have things to give, even if I had a lot of learning to do as well.

This was by now the biggest step in my career and the biggest opportunity I had taken, but it was definitely not the only one or the last one. This chance that I took would open new doors to me in the future too. Opening your eyes to the range of opportunities you face every day gives you a rich life.

Every encounter is a possibility for something previously unseen.

I don't call myself a networker, but I am connecting people. I meet people, see what they have to give each other and connect them. The connections with people have given me a lot, personally and professionally.

THE CREATE STEP TAKE OPPORTUNITIES

According to [55]Patrick Lencione, absence of trust makes a team dysfunctional, and that is also the first thing to be needed to build results. Trust is the basis of any great relationship or team. Trust is also the foundation you need to establish so you can dare to take chances.

When you trust that life can bring you opportunities, then you start seeing them around you.

As a person who takes and creates opportunities you have both a strong drive and a tendency to gain insights. Both of which [56]Rahkamo and Valpas highlight as elements of creative performance capability alongside curiosity and self-confidence. The framework Rahkamo and Valpas are painting supports my CREATE framework where I lift curiosity, self-awareness and self-value, attitude, ease, taking opportunities and enabling. These elements are inbuilt also in the Creative work 2030 report using slightly different terms.

This step is all about being active and open. Chances don't come to you if you have a closed or stagnated mindset and don't see and take the opportunities that are placed in front of you on a silver platter.

I break down "Take Opportunities" to:

A. Trust

B. See opportunities

C. Be active

D. Every encounter is a possibility for something new

E. Next level: personally – professionally – financially

F. Your way – not the traditional way

G. The creative CREATE career.

For me, every encounter is a possibility for something previously unseen or done. If you take chances, you will have all the opportunities in the world to get to the next level in your life personally, professionally and financially.

Remember that your way is the right way for you. You have now passed all the internal steps. Through curiosity, you have found your core skills and respect for yourself. By knowing yourself, you learned that what is easy for you is not easy for others. You have the attitude in place, and you know what is suitable for you. Your way is most probably not a linear, traditional career. It is something that I would call a creative CREATE career and someone else could call it a full life.

TAKING OPPORTUNITIES WITH ANNA

You have been introduced to our avatar, Anna, as a leader, but she didn't always feel like one. Like so many of us, especially when we started in leadership roles. Questioning your leadership capabilities is also a sign of maturity, because leadership is hard and no one is ever ready. It is a constant process. Anna, as we all do, was questioning her leadership because she didn't have role models that she could relate to. She always started with trust, only to sometimes be disappointed. She didn't want to lose her childlike trust and belief in wonders; she knew that by being open to see the perspective of the counterpart she would end up with win-win solutions.

Anna was seeing opportunities all around her. Her frustration was related to the cynicism she experienced from her colleagues. It required a lot of effort from her to convince the people around her that the chances she saw would impact not only the people but the business dramatically. She saw that great success would follow, so she tried. Over and over again. She showed her organisation the opportunities that were out there and things started to happen. If she hadn't acted upon her values and her beliefs, she would have felt devastated. Anna was motivated by the well-being of the organisation and its employees. She wanted to see her team, as well as the leadership team, succeed. She knew that it would take the organisation to the next level and that it would make her feel successful too.

Anna could have adapted to the situation. She could have let the opportunities pass, but that would have made her feel very disappointed with herself. Anna was doing things her way; hence it was sometimes difficult to explain to her mainstream colleagues why her way of doing business was so impactful.

THE COST OF NOT TAKING THE OPPORTUNITIES

I could have decided not to move to Latvia and take over the HR leadership of a hotel chain because it scared me. It scared me a lot, but I didn't allow myself to get paralysed by that fear. If I had not taken that chance I would have felt that I had given up before I had even started, so I wasn't willing to give my fear a chance to take hold. Jumping into the big boots of an HR director of a hotel chain was such a crazy opportunity that I could not say no.

I didn't let my husband of that time leave his job before my probation was over. I wasn't quite sure if I would be able to handle the job, so I was unsure whether I should tell everyone that I was suddenly jumping into the big shoes of an HR director of a hotel chain. Despite my insecurities, I started in the role. If I hadn't, I would have regretted not having taken the chance. Lying on your death bed, you don't regret the things you did, but the things you didn't. It brought me a lot of experiences that I would not have wanted to have missed out on.

The primary consequence of not taking opportunities is that people and companies are stuck. Seeing and bravely taking opportunities is the first of the external steps in the CREATE formula, and if you don't take opportunities, it will all remain internal. This is the first external step towards creative leadership. You may lead yourself and dream and innovate, but without the involvement of other people, internal or external partners, your actions remain minor. Take the chances you see and involve people along the way.

TAKING OPPORTUNITIES AND CREATING A PLATFORM FOR CREATIVE OPPORTUNITIES

I have been encouraging you to lead curiously and respectfully with ease and with a creative mindset. Being open to the possibilities around you makes you see opportunities everywhere. I have told you earlier in the book about starting and running a gallery in my partner's violin shop and about staging many art exhibitions there with versatile events with pleasures for all senses. In the inspiring events, I brought together people from different fields, and every event led to connections with people that led to new ideas and activities.

[57]Priya Parker says, in her book, *The Art of Gathering*, that a gathering is the conscious bringing together of people for a reason. She thinks that most of the time when we come together we are disappointed. We focus on the wrong things, like PowerPoint presentations and technical solutions, instead of focusing on what makes a group connect and a gathering matter. As much as our gatherings disappoint us, we tend to gather in the same tiresome ways, Parker says.

We live in a very hectic world where we are in a spiral of obligations. My target with the events in the violin shop gallery was to bring together passionate people from different fields to create together something previously unseen and unexperienced. I wanted to create a gathering where people got out of their loop into a space of calm and excitement. Someone said about the events we organised: "This is like from the movies!" I focused on how people feel in an event. As a host, I made sure that everyone was welcomed personally and felt seen and heard. Everyone who was part of the organisation of the event needed to feel that it gave more than it took. Each and every one of those events we organised in How Violins and Gallery Fast Creative led to something new, not only for us but for the participants: new art exhibition openings, female leader events, opportunities to perform for musicians, modelling experiences with artists, business opportunities, new collaboration and a lot more.

You may think that a violin shop is a creative environment, and it is easy to create and ideate in such a surrounding. For me it was easy, as I saw the possibilities and got people excited about the ideas and along with me on the path. I had also the luxury of organising the events with someone who trusted me and my ideas and gave me a pretty open playing field to operate in. However, in general, violin shops are made in the same mould pretty much all over the world. They are usually dark and hidden and not especially inviting environments, and the violin-making and restoration happens behind closed doors. They look and feel the same and they are not used for other fields than they were traditionally meant for. When Guy founded his violin shop, he wanted it to be open and inviting, and he has been said to have changed the culture of violin-making and the stringed instrument field in Finland. When I came along, I brought my own spice with art and gatherings with me. Even if the violin world isn't traditionally a place where such gatherings come together, it may be even more alien to think of crafting out-of-the-box experiences in the business world.

SEEING THE OPPORTUNITIES TO USE THE SKILLS AND INTERNAL NETWORKS IN A CORPORATION

Working for a global IT company I saw opportunities for individual and organisational growth and generated new ways of doing things. I liked the work environment. It seemed to be open to new ideas and had a forward-looking approach despite there being long-established corporate ways of doing things. I had brilliant colleagues around me and some of them played along and enabled the process of bringing the ideas to life. Eventually, we grew the ideas together, in collaboration, so that it became our common project, even to the extent that I can't recall who came up with what.

We started a leadership development programme using both internal and external coaches. The finance department had the target of becoming more of a forward-looking and analytical business partner rather than a reporting machine. To support this we launched the coaching programme.

We bravely kick-started the project and announced that we were looking for internal coaches and got more than 20 coaches from Finland, Sweden, Latvia, the Czech Republic and India to join the programme as coaches. They were working in different roles in the organisation – not as coaches, but in different IT, HR and development roles. All of them had coaching certification and some coaching experience outside or inside work, but the network of coaches had never been used at the IT company before.

When we had the network in place we started the programme on different levels. Firstly, we were looking to support the leadership team with developing both the strategic leadership and team building. We organised events to set targets for the programme. When I noticed that not everyone from the leadership was directly playing along, I invited anyone from the 400 strong global finance team to participate in the programme. On the first round, we drew together 30 to 40 people, with all of them having private coaching as well as being offered the chance to participate in group coaching.

With the leadership team we had external coaching partners along and we facilitated the programme with Heli Backman. Heli is definitely a creative leader whom I admire. The funny thing is that she would not think of herself as a creative person. But she is very courageous, takes opportunities, respects people, creates trust and has an incredible capability of seeing things from a fresh angle. Heli is very sharp and warm at the same time. She doesn't fear challenges and she invites new ideas. In fact, I think Heli enabled me to be the creative leader I was in that setting and, vice versa, I was feeding her creativity. Through us, it became an active dialogue between the different groups, the leadership team and the other people who had joined the programme. When the others involved were excited to advance themselves and the organisation further, it created a need and will to also develop further in the leadership, also among those who had hesitated at first. The ones who had taken the chance among the first ones, felt themselves as forerunners.

After the launch of the big coaching initiative in the finance department, with the target to improve the leadership and create a new level of finance partner support in the organisation, we launched smaller programmes with other leadership teams. The coaching and agile work initiatives started a wave of developing the leadership through self-knowledge and better understanding of the various teams, but even more so to evolve the organisation strategically.

The open organisation with a variety of expertise offered a platform for multiple opportunities. I saw the opportunities and kick-started previously unseen initiatives using the brilliant network. As it was something that hadn't been done previously in the organisation, it developed further during the process. We weren't ready when we started, but bravely started something even though we didn't know exactly what it would end up being like. Some felt uncomfortable with the ambiguity of the project and also criticised it. Others were so excited about the tools and processes that they started to study coaching themselves. Including me. I really admired the professionalism and capability of the coaches and wanted to learn similar skills too.

Corporate surroundings offer a lot more potential for development and new ways to do things than is, in general, used. Even in organisations which are not encouraging Agile ways of working, through trial, error and redirection, there may be pockets of innovation and flexibility. You can be the change in your organisation and surroundings. Start with asking what possibilities you have that you do not see because you are too used to the status quo.

Liisa Holma was one of the leaders at the IT firm whom I supported as HR. We also kick-started the development of Liisa's Client Experience team, using both coaching and Agile HR tools and collaboration partners to create a more cohesive and collaborative unit. When I asked Liisa to write a comment for this book, to be used in the Chapter "Take Opportunities", she said, "I will definitely do that, but I think I am more a make opportunities than a take opportunities person." I loved that comment. Making or creating opportunities for yourself and your surroundings requires seeing and acting on opportunities not only for yourself but also for others around you. Making Opportunities would be the next maturity phase from Taking Opportunities. It tells you that you are already far along your journey as a creative leader. You are the enabler I talk about in the next Chapter.

Guest writer

LIISA HOLMA

CEO Un-known, Author, Podcast Host

I have always been curious – one of my favourite pastimes is learning. I am hungry for new experiences and get bored with repeated work quickly. When this happens, I become lazy and, honestly, not very engaged with my job. Thus, finding something new is actually a necessity for me.

This doesn't mean that I'm not afraid; I've often thought about why I have put myself in a particular position. There was also a point in my life where I felt I had to divert my career. I had been in a responsible role and failed. I realised that my failure mostly had to do with the fact that I had taken the role because of its prestige, not because it was something I was interested in. I had to reinvent myself professionally to find an area where I could combine my strengths, ambitions, and know-how.

I started to learn about the things and topics that I wanted to work with. For me, writing is one of the best ways of learning, so I started to write on social media about what I learned and thought. My writings generated conversations with people on social media, which gave me perspectives, and I identified opportunities to grasp.

I only recently realised that taking or actually making opportunities is one of my strengths. It is my parachute if everything else fails. I believe that by applying my experience in a new context, I can find new ways forward. Taking opportunities often requires following your passion, not a career path. You cannot expect that your salary will continuously increase and your career will progress while you explore and learn new things. It's a side hustle, or a sidestep. Not all hustles are opportunities, but something that, at first, seems like a "waste of time" might become useful going forward.

HOW TO TAKE OPPORTUNITIES

Taking opportunities is about trusting them to come to you.

Having the attitude of bravely seeing and taking opportunities will make it look easy for you.

It looks easy because you are active and have your sensitive antennas up all the time. You connect with people, see opportunities instead of obstacles and are brave enough to take on new things. You do not only see opportunities but also create them, both for yourself and others. That's why people like to be around you. Magic happens in your presence.

Trust your intuition question

Take Opportunities: What opportunities do I see in my life now (at work, in my community and in my personal life)?

Gift yourself and others

Dare to have an attitude that giving to others will in turn give to you. I am convinced that by giving without asking for anything in return you will receive back in different ways. By supporting others you will notice that you will be supported too. Help a younger colleague and they might remember you when you are looking for a job later. Support someone who got fired and you may be given a helping hand when you need it.

A sparkly marketing manager lady who I admired told me, when I had recently graduated, that it makes her happy to see young, talented and ambitious women like me. Later, when I noticed on LinkedIn that she was looking for a job in her 50s, I contacted her and wrote that I hoped she still felt like the successful and brilliant woman I remembered. I have, as a recruiting manager and many times within HR, witnessed how professional people suddenly shrink after they are at a certain age or are unemployed. I wanted to remind her of her brilliance, and she was very taken and wanted to meet me. When I was recently divorced, a friend of mine sent her 18-year-old son to wash all my windows, which was a huge job. Later, I offered career coaching, to both the mother and son.

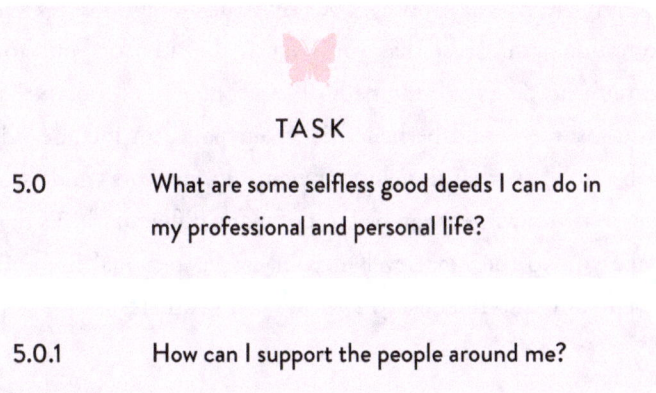

TASK

| 5.0 | What are some selfless good deeds I can do in my professional and personal life? |

| 5.0.1 | How can I support the people around me? |

> **5.0.2** How can I see and take opportunities around me and create possibilities and opportunities for myself and others?

Trust yourself and others

Even if you are in a place on your path that doesn't feel fulfilling for you, trust that what you are doing now is the step you need to move forward on your journey towards something that feels more like you. The steps during my career that didn't feel like they were mine taught me the most about me and my values.

> **5.1** How do I define myself if I do not define myself through my work or career?

Answering the above question gets you to another level in your process. You may not immediately get job offers that feel like dream career opportunities, but they can be significant steps on your path. Trust that your way is the way for you. You do not need to walk the path of someone else or a path that you assume would be beneficial. Your path can include side jobs, hobbies, charities, entrepreneurship, networks and associations. Your career can be built of many different blocks that take you to the next level in your career, personal life and, eventually, also financially. How do you get there?

5.2 What are the elements that build my CREATE career?

Challenge yourself and others

We talked about giving and trusting. What more is needed to nail it? Every encounter is a possibility for something new. When someone offers you an opportunity, be brave, take it and make it yours. Sometimes, when you face opportunities they are so big that the fear overwhelms you. It is said that if an opportunity doesn't frighten you, then it is not big enough for you. Don't give in to the fear, but dance with it. Bravery is not being fearless – it is fearing something and doing it anyway.

As Liisa Holma mentions, you do not always directly get better pay or even as much as you are used to getting if you change your path and try something new and potentially more fulfilling. We know the concept of the so-called gilded cage that many of us sit in. People who reached a very good level of income at a young age, or during their career, might not dare to take the sidesteps or new career steps because their life is built based on a certain income level that they are used to. How can you say yes to inspiring opportunities anyway? How can you build a CREATE career that looks and feels like your own?

5.3 How can I get elements of my dream tasks into my life while working with what I do now (if you are not in your ideal role or organisation, or if that doesn't feel enough for you)?

5.3.1 How will I create such circumstances that I dare to jump outside my box or comfort zone?

Do you have some long-awaited dreams? A dream to get a new role or job? A dream to become a member of a board of directors or an advisory board? A dream to write a book, start a blog or a vlog? A dream to found a company of your own? A dream to start a podcast? A dream to organise events? A dream to start selling your art? You name it.

5.4 What is holding me back?

The things that mostly hold us back are time, money, insecurity and procrastination. It may also be a lack of some skills that are required for the thing that you are dreaming of. Maybe you would like to found a company but fear the accounting. Or you would like to be a board member but do not have the legal skills.

> **5.4.1** Firstly, ask yourself: Do I need to have all the skills myself or can I partner up with someone, buy the service or learn new skills?

> **5.4.2** Secondly, ask yourself: Do I need more time or money, or could I start doing something alongside my current job?

> **5.4.3** Thirdly, ask yourself: What if I am enough? What if my skills are exactly the ones needed to fulfil a leadership team, board of advisors or something else that I am targeting?

For me, writing this book was a dream that I never seemed to have time for. I did already do plenty of things aside from my main job, like organising events and coaching, but writing the book still felt like such a big task to take on that it was constantly postponed, year after year. In autumn 2021 after one and a half years of Covid restrictions, and no face-to-face events organised, I suddenly saw a post on LinkedIn about a writing group. This was the opportunity that I had been waiting for, and four months later I had written about 40,000 words, even with a full-time job. What would be a similar opportunity for you?

You can use your beautiful notebook to write down your dreams and start keeping your eyes open for possibilities. Once again, look into what is easy for you. Find what you are good at and which parts you need to find support with. Spot your Ikigai to find what you should go for: a) what you are good at, b) what you love, c) what the world needs, and d) what you can be paid for (more in Chapter 7: Ease). You can also implement smaller dreams of yours. Something that introduces a spark to your life and career but doesn't necessarily change the whole package. Everything you do advances you, either professionally or as a human being. You can be merciful to yourself. Also, the things you do not burn for are on your path for a reason. It is rarely clear until later why that was an important step on your path. Looking back, everything seems so much clearer than when you were plodding along your path.

Whatever you do, do it like you. And believe in you!

If you are looking for a new job, be honest about what you bring with you. Alongside your skills, expertise and experience, tell them what your family circumstances look like. When I was interviewed for an HR leadership role in a law firm, I told them that I was divorced and I was part of the time living alone with two children and responsible for running the household on my own. If that would not have been OK for my employer, I would not have wanted to work with them.

Being younger, I was very much thinking about what would be a suitable dress code for an interview. I never wore red, so I would not be considered to be "too much". Later, I thought that if they cannot accept me in a red dress, it is not going to be the right place for me. I love wearing red.

Be you. Put your cards on the table: If they don't want you with your full package, then you do not share their values and don't want to work with them. This might be easier said than done if you are without a job and desperate to get one. Sometimes it is better to wait longer to get what feels right, but sometimes you just take something to come further along your path. Whatever is suitable for you in the circumstances you are living through is the key. If you are the only caregiver in the family, understandably, you need to get the food on the table. But even so, you must follow your dreams. Any one of us knows, though, that every organisation has its challenges, and we will have our challenges operating within them. Again, remembering what your value is and operating from a position where you respect both yourself and others will leave you feeling more confident about your moves.

I have a dream to make leadership teams, advisory boards and boards of directors more diverse, whether in regards to gender, origin, education or age, but also when thinking about creativity. Luckily, you can find others who are like-minded. LinkedIn is one good place to connect with like-minded people. I have found new friends there too, just by commenting and praising someone's successes. Helene Auramo shares that vision of more diverse boards with me, and she has founded a platform for bringing together impact companies and professional leaders. Her passion is to bring more diversity into advisory boards through the Prönö platform. Maybe you will sign up too?

The ideas above support you on your path towards taking opportunities, but you might need a professional coach to support you further in your development. A coach can help you to find the insights that you need on your path. The 'Take Opportunities' Chapter already introduces the idea of enabling through giving and creating opportunities for others. We are digging more deeply into enabling as we move on to Chapter 10: Enable.

THE KEY TAKEAWAYS OF CHAPTER 9: TAKE OPPORTUNITIES

In this Chapter you have learned:

- Every encounter is a possibility for something previously unseen.

- When you trust that life can bring you opportunities, you start seeing them around you.

- If you take chances, then you have all the opportunity in the world to get to the next level in your life personally, professionally and financially.

- Lying on your death bed, you will not regret the things you did, but the things you didn't do.

- Dare to have an attitude that giving will give back to you. Whatever you do, do it like you. And believe in you!

CHAPTER 10

ENABLE – BE THE CREATIVE LEADER

"Standing at the crossroads
Trying to read the signs
To tell me which way I should go
To find the answer
And all the time I know
Plant your love and let it grow."

"LET IT GROW" BY [58]ERIC CLAPTON

ENABLING CHANGE BY GIVING A NUDGE

In Chapter 7, I discussed how moving the Daydream statue and the Children's Dream events were examples of projects that were done with ease. Being an open network, the Kannelmäki movement did not have any official leaders. However, influencing and making a change requires people who have leadership skills, communication skills and the capability to turn dreams into action. It requires someone who sees possibilities, takes opportunities and enables and encourages people to take responsibility for their surroundings.

We said, "You are the Kannelmäki movement. How do you want to make Kannelmäki an even better place to live, work and visit?" The old-fashioned neighbourhood associations were mainly focusing on what was wrong and trying to make small changes in the surroundings that they thought would be suitable. Instead, we opened it out, saying that everyone was creating the movement, and when people had ideas for improvements, we said, "Great idea, do it!"

That led to many Facebook groups being founded: recycling, helping in the neighbourhood, children's activities, local farmer markets etc. It also led to many local activities where people were knitting together, dancing, creating art, organising pop-up restaurants. When someone had an idea for an improvement, we said, "What a great idea! What if you wrote to the Minister about it?" And after a while, they posted proudly in the Facebook group that they had written a letter to the Minister of the Interior. Taking responsibility and action made people proud, not only of themselves but of their neighbourhood too.

We had a small group of activists who actively defined the messages, encouraged positive discussions and actions and encouraged people to act upon their ideas. The buzz around the neighbourhood, which had previously been seen as less attractive, became so intense that I was invited to speak at international seminars, to the communications managers of the city of Helsinki and in a Helsinki University lecture series about neighbourhoods that have been actively branded. I was even invited to talk to the bishop of Helsinki, Irja Askola, and her team, and Irja Askola said, "I am very impressed! What you are doing in your neighbourhood is what I want the Church to be in the future." She saw the value of empowering people and enabling them to take action. She also commented that good things happen through friction. When there are altering ideas that collide then something new can happen.

Guest writer

KIMMO RÖNKÄ

CEO, Future Living Specialist, Neighbourhood Designer, Founder of the Kannelmäki Movement

I always get inspired by different people with versatile backgrounds. For example, when I was the CEO of a social housing company, I wanted to hire people with no experience in social housing. I didn't want to have old routines with closed minds. Finally, we got great people from the hotel business, cruise hospitality and modern retail. We also hired a person with no expertise but a super great personality.

If you want to succeed in the future you have to get out of your own box. And it is easier to step out of the box together with a team with different personalities and ideas.

The Kannelmäki movement was a perfect out-of-the-box adventure. People had various backgrounds but they shared a love for their neighbourhood. When we were launching the movement we had a group of people with experiences from the music, food, literature and culture industries. The idea of the movement was to ask people what they wanted to do for their neighbourhood, not doing it for them. As a result, we shared a lot of knowledge, skills, passion and dreams – and a lot of fun!

To get something to happen, you need two things: First, you need goodwill – people who believe in what they are doing – and a common understanding. People who see where we are heading. In many projects, this takes the biggest chunk of the time. But after having common goodwill, then you need a strong desire to get it done.

Enabling leadership is about creating that goodwill together with the people. It means that everybody knows that they play an important role and that they are valuable and have something to share with others.

WHAT IS THE CREATE STEP ENABLE ABOUT?

Enable is the last of the CREATE steps and the other of the two external steps of the formula. When you master all these steps, you are a full-blooded Creative Leader. However, it doesn't mean that you couldn't practise creative leadership without mastering all of these elements. You can be a good way towards becoming a creative leader long before you master them all. Awareness is the key. The right mindset helps you in any situation to see things more broadly and find new solutions.

1. C – Curiosity

2. R – Respect yourself and others (will too)

3. E – Ease and effortlessness

4. A – Attitude and acceptance

5. T – Take opportunities

6. E – Enable

Enabling is all about bringing people together to create something previously unseen.

> *Creativity is not a heroic myth.*
> *It is about doing things together.*

I am talking about you enabling the growth of your team members, but it refers just as much to any collaboration with your peers. In the [59]Deloitte Insights report about social enterprises it is said that organisations have become more team focused, but this change is not yet seen in leadership teams. We need to build on our strengths and create teams that are stronger together. With this book, I want to show you that change is possible, both in your personal life and organisation.

> *You do not need to travel the world to find the most*
> *creative people in the world. You can start from*
> *within and then enlarge the circle to the*
> *people who surround you.*

Every encounter is a possibility for something new.

I break down the Enable step to:

A. Be humane

B. Be present

C. Be a connector

D. Create (unofficial) teams

E. Excite

F. Energise

G. Encourage

H. Enable (I break down the four last Es further in this Chapter).

It all starts with being humane. When you have empathy for people, you see them as individuals who have their own values and experiences. You can see them for what they are, and they feel safe to try, fail, re-direct and do again. Creativity thrives in surroundings where you do not fear mistakes. Many working cultures do not encourage taking risks, but there might be pockets of psychological safety even within organisations that do not encourage risk taking and creative ideas.

BEING THE CONNECTOR

As a leader, you have the responsibility to be a safe space for your team. The one they can lean on. Being openly you supports you too. Translating your natural way of doing things whilst also being transparent about your weaknesses – your weaknesses will not be some well-known secret, but instead something that your team knows that you are aware of and acting upon. This makes you vulnerable and demands a lot of courage, but it gives you strength too. Because you are not hiding your development areas. You should be open about them from the start. Hiding things takes a lot of energy. Use your energy to support and create. Some working cultures do not support this at all, but the change needs to start somewhere. Be that change.

"The true value of networking doesn't come from how many people we meet, but rather how many people we can introduce to each other."

[60]**SIMON SINEK**

That's why I call it connecting rather than networking. Surround yourself with people who have different skill sets and motivations and together you will be more. Connect people. Find collaboration partners who can support your targets. Within all the organisations where I have worked, I have built unofficial teams around me. I love to be surrounded by people who complement my features and my skills. Get to know people and their strengths, and listen. Be present. According to [61]Caroline Webb, hundreds of studies have compared the levels and causes for happiness, and money matters but not that much. What's more important, research found, is the quality of people's relationships, Webb says. And according to her we do not always need to talk to our nearest and dearest or to our co-workers to reap useful social benefits. Even the tiniest sense of connection with fellow human beings can boost us. It has been found that both introverts and extroverts felt happier on days when they had more interactions.

THE FOUR E'S OF ENABLING

The final steps of the Enable formula, I have drawn into another formula. The 4 E´s: Excite, Energise, Encourage and Enable. These steps, taken with ease, will take you further towards Creative Leadership.

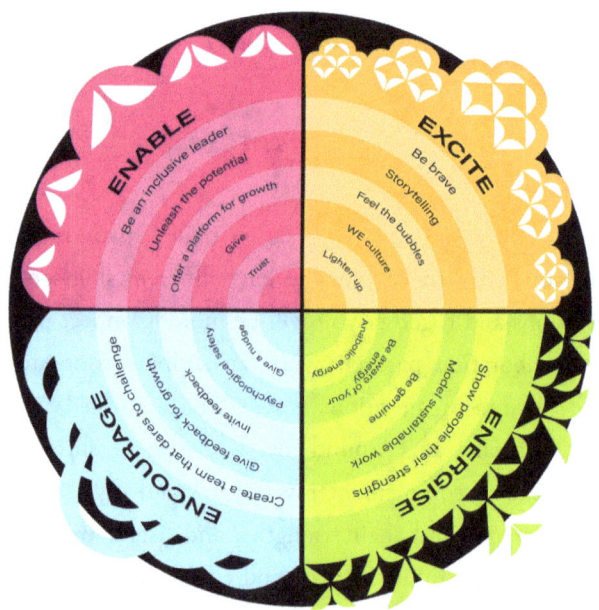

Picture 5. The circle of the 4 E's

Excite	Energise	Encourage	Enable
Lighten up	Anabolic energy – not catabolic energy	Give a nudge	Trust – it all begins with trust
WE culture	Leading energy: what kind of energy do you bring to situations? Awareness	Psychological safety	Give without asking in return – giving will give back
Spark – something new is going to come	Be genuine – be truthful, open and vulnerable	Ask and invite feedback	Offer a platform for growth
Storytelling	Take care of your energy – model sustainable work	Give feedback that enables growth	Unleash the potential in others and yourself, US
Be brave	Show your (unofficial) team members what they are good at – mirroring	Create a team that is not afraid to challenge	See synergies – be an inclusive leader

The elements of creative leadership can be used in any surroundings. They can be used in official work areas, in hobbies, in charity organisations, within open networks and even with your family and friends. People will want to be around you if you radiate the positive energy of an enabler. Notice that people will want to get your energy and the key thing is to make sure that you have energy for yourself. Otherwise, you will not have the energy to give to others.

As an enabler, you will shine and spark and create a culture where everyone feels valued. You are brave and people look up to you. Since you will be the North Star taking people and teams forward, you carry a lot of responsibility. Make sure you act from a place of [62]anabolic energy, rather than catabolic energy. That means that you do not look for someone to blame and do not act as if you were a victim. Rather you take responsibility for your actions, model healthy and sustainable work, and encourage and coach the people around you. You also don't control others to reach your targets, but collaborate, share information and experience and look into the future. But you as an enabling creative leader need energy too, so seek out people who radiate good vibes, like [63]Webb suggests. When you get enough anabolic energy, you have energy and resilience to also try to get on board the ones who need more encouraging and persuasion.

Model sustainable work. There are many ways to show that you work efficiently and creatively without working 24/7. No one can work all the time. We also need to have the space to think and create. Creativity is not at all contradictory to efficiency. They are not opposites. Creativity can bring efficiency when you find new ways of doing things in a more timely and structured matter. You also tend to hear people saying that they do not have time for creativity. **Creativity doesn't take time. It is a mindset**. It is a way of thinking. It is good to block slots in your calendar for planning and doing things out of the box, but in my experience, the creative ideas are mostly born in quick, unofficial discussions that were not especially designed for creating. The creativity is inspired in collaboration with people who feel safe and inspired. Creative ideas can also spark in your head any time of the day, just by observing, connecting and thinking.

Working for an advertising and design agency, I noticed how there were, within the organisation, different subcultures related to creativity. The advertising agency part of the organisation was more determined to think that all processes kill creativity. They thought that creativity needs space; hence we had, among other gadgets, a ping-pong table in the office to create that environment. But the design part of the organisation was used to structured processes and they thought that that would bring time and space for creativity. We experience and express creativity in different ways. Your task as a creative leader is to join these dots together. To connect the people around you to create something together.

THE PLAYGROUND OF CREATIVE LEADERSHIP

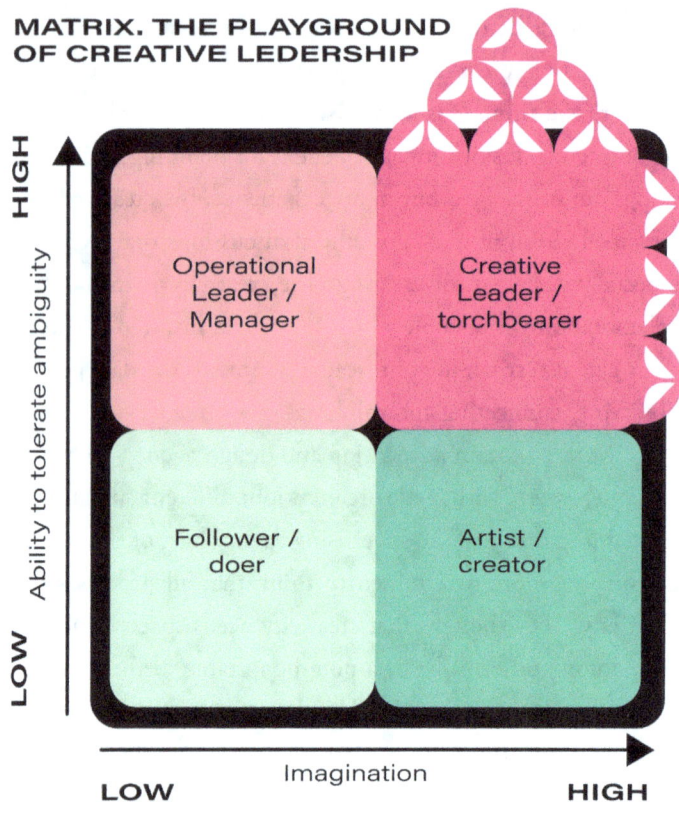

MATRIX. THE PLAYGROUND OF CREATIVE LEDERSHIP

- Y-axis: Ability to tolerate ambiguity (LOW to HIGH)
- X-axis: Imagination (LOW to HIGH)
- High ambiguity / Low imagination: Operational Leader / Manager
- High ambiguity / High imagination: Creative Leader / torchbearer
- Low ambiguity / Low imagination: Follower / doer
- Low ambiguity / High imagination: Artist / creator

The creative leader is the visionary who helps other people along the way. They are the torchbearers who can lead both people and organisations towards a brighter future. The creative leader needs to be comfortable with ambiguity and they have high imagination. An operational leader can be comfortable with ambiguity, but they are more unfamiliar with imagination. The doers and followers do not feel comfortable with ambiguity, imagination or change, but we do need them along on our journey so we can get things done. You can lead people to execute creative initiatives even if they wouldn't be the torchbearers themselves. And people can be in different phases on their creative journey. The artists are not necessarily the leaders of the initiatives, but they have a lot to give. You just need to be open to listening and making them feel heard, so that you can get the creative ideas and people on board.

HOW TO ENGAGE PEOPLE AND LEAD ENERGY

The enabler gets the people with them. To know how to get the people to follow you, you need to be open to looking out for the energy in people and organisations. It is not only about making sure that people eat, sleep, rest and exercise enough, even though filling our basic needs is the base for having energy. It is about mastering your energy use, knowing your strengths and motivators as well as the strengths and motivators of the people surrounding you. Talking about leading energy can sound fluffy and vague, but it is actually a core element in leadership. [64]Heli Backman and Nina Karlsson have looked deeply into leading energy with their Energy Coaching company. They say it can be a fast track toward changes compared with changing the culture which requires a lot of time. I have had the pleasure of working with them, for a long time in many instances, and I have also participated in their Energy Leader Trainer® Programme.

Leading the energy of people starts with knowing their strengths, building teams with people who have complementary skills and motivators and making sure that everyone has enough tasks on their plate that are energising for them. We all know that all jobs and roles also involve things that do not inspire us as much. But if we constantly do things that are not inspiring us, it takes a lot of energy. As a leader, I try to make sure that everyone has as much as possible of the tasks that are inspiring them. Saana Rossi says in her text in this book that she has done similar things with her teams (for example, built job descriptions on the basis of the motivators of her team members). I believe that it is the way to create committed teams and team members. The amount of work is not usually the thing that burdens most, unless the load is over the top. What burdens is the feeling that you cannot influence your work: if you do not see the whole picture and do not understand your role or part in the process, and if you feel that you cannot plan your time. It is, of course, not always possible to find tasks that inspire everyone, but a lot can be done by looking at things more broadly. In smaller organisations, you sometimes just have to do what needs to be done. However, also in those surroundings, you can develop things and bring in new ideas and feel that you made an impact. Leading energy is about optimising your energy use.

[65]Teresa M. Amabile says that individual creativity exists as a function of three components: expertise, creative-think-

ing skills and motivation. She says that the first two are more difficult and time consuming to influence, but it is easier to influence someone's intrinsic motivation – and the results are immediate. To be able to influence the motivation of people, you need to know them and their motivators and energisers. That is something I opened up more in Chapter 6: Respect yourself and others. According to Amabile, you can influence people's intrinsic motivation by e.g. matching the right people with the right assignments, giving people freedom within the company goals, allocating appropriate amounts of time and resources and letting the people know that what they do matters. If people are motivated they also feel energised.

As a leader or manager, my task is to enable the growth of my team members. The paradox of leadership, as well as parenting, is that if we are the enablers that we need to be, we end up eventually making ourselves unnecessary. That can feel scary. To be honest, we will rarely become totally unnecessary. If you have progressed far enough as a leader that you can enable and help others grow, you have so much knowledge that people will keep learning from you. But we can also learn from the younger or less experienced ones. Hence the concept of reverse mentoring is clever. It is a win-win to learn from what the different personalities or generations can teach each other. The main thing is to find the motivators and strengths of the individuals and work in collaboration so that we can get great results together. Succeeding energises too.

Leading the organisation's energy takes us a big step further. Making sure that the individuals and teams are mainly feeling good and come from anabolic energy whilst collaborating with each other is, of course, the first step. Organisations can have different energies. Some companies have a very positive and forward-looking approach, which welcomes development and new ideas. Other organisations have a culture to shoot down ideas. Which one do you think is more fruitful? To be critical is not a bad thing. It is how you criticise that matters. Are you looking for new solutions or are you just complaining? Are you taking responsibility for your actions and behaviour or blaming others? Leading organisation energy starts from within. What do I bring to the table? How do I interact with my colleagues, or greet them in the morning? After you have looked at yourself in the mirror, you can start observing the behaviour of your colleagues. Not leading energy is not an option, as Heli Backman says.

STORIES ABOUT TRUST AND CREATIVITY

Storytelling is a brilliant tool to inspire. I have noticed in practice how easy it is to get people to follow you if you have an interesting story to tell. People want to be involved when they experience something meaningful. When you create a team that is not afraid to fail, magic happens. Some ideas do fail, but if you stop trying, neither you nor the organisation will evolve. Asking for and giving feedback is essential for development. When you give feedback, you should remember the negative bias, which is so significant that you have to give 6 to 10 times more positive feedback than negative or constructive feedback to balance it to a neutral level. In my experience, people want to exceed your expectations when they get a lot of positive feedback. You end up with inspired people who want to do their best when you give a lot of positive affirmation.

Trust is the key to success in collaboration. Many organisations write policies that sound like someone is expected to misuse their rights. The best organisations are based on trust. They know that the trust will sometimes be misused, but it is a risk they are willing to take for the upside of having that trust. As an example, this policy has been used in Futurice: they all have their own credit card and they are trusted to use them for the right purposes. If someone thinks that it is bringing in money to work from a pool house terrace in Spain, you can buy tickets to Spain with your company credit card. People who feel valued want to give their best. This is valid in any collaboration in private and professional life.

The CEO of Vincit USA, [66]Ville Houttu, launched the "CEO for a day" concept after one of his employees had named the heading of an appraisal discussion calendar invitation "xx for CEO". To the surprise of his subordinate, Ville actually gave him the chance to be CEO for one day. During that day he had unlimited budget to make one decision for the organisation. The only condition for the money use was that it needed to be beneficial to the company and its people. The first decision was to get beanbags to the office. It was executed even though the actual CEO, Ville himself, hates beanbags. He is about two metres tall and finds beanbags incredibly uncomfortable. Despite the fact that the first employee decision as CEO of the day was unsuccessful from the perspective of the CEO, Ville Houttu decided to continue with the CEO of the day concept on a monthly basis.

The previous CEO of the day always chooses the CEO of the day of the following month. In this way, the employees genuinely create the company culture with their own decisions. Even though the budget is unlimited, it is such a huge responsibility to carry, that no one has gone over the top with the money usage. It also shows to the employees how difficult it is to make decisions that everybody can be happy about – maybe even impossible. This is an example of extreme trust that actually ended up growing the business significantly. Not all organisations are ready to give their employees this kind of trust, but maybe they should…

What is your story that people want to follow? As an enabler, you offer the people a platform for growth. Unleashing the potential in you and the people around you, you will see the synergies and trust that giving will give back to you.

WHY IS THE ENABLE STEP ESPECIALLY IMPORTANT FOR ANNA?

Our avatar, Anna, is a full-blooded creative leader by now. She has developed along the journey, as you have too. She started by being insecure despite pretty good self-esteem. That is the huge contradiction that pretty much every leader lives with. It requires bravery to get to a leadership role. It requires attitude, persistence and different kinds of skills. But the higher up in rank a person rises, the bigger the case of imposter syndrome they can develop. It isn't stopped by getting another respected leadership role. Anna's big challenge during her journey has been that she hasn't met leaders she would like to use as models. Her way has felt so different from the leadership styles she has experienced that she was even questioning if she was fit to be a leader.

Anna had built up her self-esteem around external matters, but when she started digging into herself, finding her strengths and goals, then she could breathe more easily. She noticed that the things that were easy for her were not easy for others. She realised that she has a lot to give to this world and she started by creating change in her close surroundings. Anna noticed that the more she respected herself, the more she was respected by others.

The Enable step is especially important for Anna as it gives her a framework for the kind of leader she wants to be. She wants to be an enabler who supports people in their careers to become something suitable for them. She wants to enable organisations to advance and succeed. Anna has become the role model she wanted to find and is building this up in others who she can count on to extend her ethos. She may find role models for future growth among those she has inspired. If Anna had had a clear picture of the enabling leader in her mind before, then she could have cut her journey a little bit shorter, and the road home would have been less bumpy. But she needed to do it her way to find out what she knows now. Reading this book can make your path towards becoming an enabling, creative leader smoother.

THE COST OF NOT BEING AN ENABLER

If our avatar, Anna, chose to not be the enabling leader she always wanted to be, she would feel bad about herself. She would also not get her team onside with her. She might end up not being a leader at all, at work or in her life overall.

The primary consequence of not taking Step 6: Enable into action is that many things that were planned then never happen in reality. The first four steps are more about yourself and your growth. Step 5: Take Opportunities already involves other parties and enabling, but it is still primarily about you noticing the opportunities. Step 6 is giving birth to the creative leader. It generates actions together with people. It brings ideas and thoughts into reality in collaboration with other people. Without living and breathing Step 6: Enable, Anna is not the leader she wants to be. Hence this step is the ultimate and critical one for you to finalise your journey with.

We know, of course, that no one is ever ready as a leader or a human being. It requires constant awareness and work to become a better version of oneself. Some days feel more in the weeds than others. Sometimes the soul sings with the delight of getting things forward, showing up as a role model and leader for the people around you. Other times you need someone to lead and support you. That is being a human being. Part of this journey is to also show that any leader is a human being and needs human interaction, support, acceptance and also acknowledgement.

LEADING BY GIVING SPACE – ENABLING

As a leader, I try to give space to the people around me. I am very assertive and I have needed to practise listening, hearing and giving space. My coaching skills support me in asking questions instead of giving answers. I think that my duty as a manager and a leader is to offer a platform for growth. I have a wonderful, respectful and gracious team around me. My team also knows my strengths and weaknesses, and I am very open about what I am good at and what I prefer to have support with. I love people with different strengths around me. That makes us a brilliant team together.

I like to give responsibility and support along the way. Oftentimes we hear that managers are too busy to instruct properly or to coach forward. My own experience is that each time I took proper time to support someone or coach them, it gave me more time and space further down the line. My target is to be the enabler, both at work and in private life. But it takes leadership maturity to know that you are never ready.

THE GREAT RESIGNATION – HOW PEOPLE GIVE THEIR BEST WHEN THEY FEEL RESPECTED

I am happy that we had such an open and honest relationship within my team that when a team member was looking for a new job, she told me about it many months in advance, and I was supporting her through the job search. She didn't leave because she didn't want to work with us. She left because she wanted to grow further in areas she couldn't focus on in her current role or within our organisation. As long as she worked with me, I was trying to give her as many challenges as possible in fields that would develop her further. But I knew all along that she had plans that could not be fulfilled where she was. She gave her best until the very end of the working relationship. There were no hard feelings when she left. I was happy for her to get those new challenges that she wanted, and we were both sad that we would not be working together anymore.

Throughout the years, and whilst working in many organisations, I have met many managers who didn't want their (best) team members to leave and were, sometimes, even personally hurt when someone moved to a new role within the organisation or left for new challenges elsewhere. This could be even to the extent that they would put down the person after they left and wanted to pretend that it was better that the person had left, as they weren't any good anyway. As leaders and managers, we have to understand that if we do not let people grow, they will leave. Internal moves should therefore be welcomed when they involve a possibility for growth for a great employee. We do not own our employees and team members, as we do not own our children. We need to support them to grow and enable it. As long as the organisation can offer opportunities for growth and a good atmosphere then people will want to stay. But we cannot assume that anyone will stay forever. We can't take our team members for granted, just as we cannot take our spouses or friends for granted. Even if we do know that someone has different progression plans than our organisation can offer, they will give their best as long as they are working with us if they feel respected. When someone leaves an organisation it is usually a win-win situation because, at the end of the day, they would not be motivated if they were not able to do what they were dreaming of doing.

We are facing now, in many fields around the world, what is being called The Great Resignation. A lot of people are leaving their jobs. In many discussions internally and externally, it seems that the impact of Covid, with remote work and lockdowns, has diluted the glue within organisations that keeps us together as a team: fewer face-to-face contacts, no parties and far fewer unofficial gatherings. Working has become more efficient in some ways but, at the same time, it is less personal.

I hear many people say that they could work as well for some other company from their living room or their summer cabin. Remote work was common in many organisations before Covid, but as the whole world (meaning the population doing information work and the parts of the world where there was a remote working infrastructure in place) was suddenly forced to become fully remote, then many people failed to keep up with the changes. This period that has been impacted by Covid has brought us different restrictions than we have had before, with many of us having seen very few people in person. Even though we have moved to hybrid work from the total remote working times, more time alone has made people reflect upon their values and look for meaning in their lives.

COLOUR AND COMMUNALITY IN OUR NEIGHBOURHOOD

I started the Enable Chapter with examples of how we were enabling change in my neighbourhood, Kannelmäki, when I lived there. Kimmo Rönkä, who founded the Kannelmäki movement, is a brilliant enabler. He talks to people, inspires them, and gives them a nudge so that they end up executing his creative ideas.

At the beginning of my Kannelmäki movement activism, I wanted to participate in every initiative. I was very much involved with the activities that I initiated and innovated, and I was hands-on as I led them through to completion. However, along the way, I noticed that I could not do it all. I was the initiator of the huge Daydream statue being moved to our neighbourhood. We met Helsinki city architects. I gathered together groups of people who were interested in bringing more colour to our area. I contacted groups of street art artists. I contacted schools and suggested that we would collaborate. Eventually, murals and other forms of street art started to come up in many places in Kannelmäki without me actually doing anything. I had just given them the nudge.

When I noticed that a big mural was being painted at the end of my road, I went to talk with the artist. A man who had been in one of the first meetings I had arranged to bring colour to our neighbourhood was also there, following the live painting of the mural. He was an introverted engineer and he had told us in the meeting: "I don't know how to do these things. I am here only to listen." And it was eventually him who initiated the painting of the mural at the end of the blockhouses where he lived. He told me that he had contacted an organisation to get a mural there and reminded me that it had originally been my idea to have a mural at that exact location. I didn't even remember that I had suggested painting a mural on the walls of that building, but he had picked it up and initiated the whole thing. The person who had told me that he could not do these things had eventually done it. I was in awe. The point wasn't for me to do all of it. I had kick-started something that started to live its own life. How empowering it must have felt for the young man to see the beautiful colourful painting at the end of his house, knowing that he had initiated it! There were more and more pieces of street art coming up. The colouring had started and the people were proud of being a part of it.

Years later, I had conversations with eighth and ninth graders who were doing work experience training for a week at the law firm where I was leading the HR team. I was meeting them for discussions and encouragement. We had started a school collaboration to bring more diversity to the law field in Finland and we chose Kannelmäki elementary school as one of our partnering schools. One of the girls said she wanted to become a lawyer, but she wasn't sure whether she could make it. I managed to convince her that anything is possible when you work towards your dreams. The discussions with the young trainees felt very meaningful, as I thought that I might have had a life-changing discussion with those young girls. One of the girls said, "It's my dream to become a leader."

"Great," I said. "Go girl! You can absolutely become that."

I told the young girls that I used to be a Kannelmäki movement activist when I lived there. I told them about the colour I wanted to bring to the neighbourhood and how we had launched a theme of Dreaming Big in Kannelmäki. One of the girls was so taken. She said, "Wow! Did you do it?! I see those murals and the statue all the time and it was your idea. Wow!" She was gasping.

It gave us a common ground and we had a very open and honest conversation about studying, working and living. There we were, a 15-year-old girl who came to Finland as a refugee and a 45-year-old Finnish HR Leader, having a connection through the use of colour in the neighbourhood. At the end of the week, she got great feedback from the people she had worked with, and I heard later from her teacher that the discussion had been very motivational for her and had given her a real purpose to go on and do well at school too.

HOW TO BE AN ENABLER

Today's business world is not about hiding your ideas and products from your competitors, instead it is about collaborating with different parties. We talk about ecosystems and networks that are created to make an impact together. The impact can be improved by aligning organisations and people. It is about supporting and leading people with different professional and cultural backgrounds. How can you build networks and ecosystems around you to support growth and creativity? Get back to the beginning of the CREATE formula: live and breathe curiosity. Have an open mind and be interested in the people around you. Listen to them and you will find out that your surroundings have a lot to give. See the possibilities and encourage the people around you to create the change with you. Put your hands in the mud and inspire people to follow.

You may ask, how am I supposed to inspire? If you have a vision, tell your story about it. If you can create an interesting enough vision of where we are going together, which feels like a win-win, then you will have people with you on the path.

Not everyone is going to be with you right away. Some are going to challenge you. Listen to them because they most probably have something important to say, something you should focus on whilst making the plan better. Some people are inspired by the exciting tingle of the new, some may follow when there are more people involved, and some will fight the change until the end.

Trust your intuition question

Enable: How can I encourage people around me to use their creativity?

Gift yourself and your team

The Enable step is not only about you anymore. That suits you because you know that to make a change you need to have the people with you. You are driven by a desire to make an impact and the impact is created together with people. The team doesn't necessarily mean an official team from your organisation. It can also be a group of friends, your family or a loose network or ecosystem of people who share a common goal.

TASK

6.0   What unofficial teams do I have around me (or can I create around me)?

We have worked on all the previous steps before this. By now, you will feel much more confident that you have things to give to the world by being yourself. You do not need to try to copy others to be respected. When you respect yourself, others will too. Show yourself and your team the value of each individual. Celebrate what each of you can bring to the table. Be grateful for your gifts and thank the people you work with. I have experienced, as a leader, that there is a great need for acknowledgement. I hear in all engagement surveys and exit discussions that people feel that they want to get more feedback and want to feel valued.

6.1 How can I show the value of my team members?

6.1.1 How can I thank my team members?

People want to be heard and seen. The easiest and cheapest way to gift people is to say thank you. When you believe that your unofficial or official team can do miracles, they will.

Trust yourself and your team

As a leader, it is my obligation to create a space for growth. Showing up as you, honestly and openly, creates a trusting space with psychological safety for the people around you. Even in organisations where psychological safety is not the norm, you can bring that to your team.

Be part of the team. [67]Siamäk Naghian, CEO of Genelec, said in The Leadership Forum for Creativity and Innovation: "Creativity lives in every human being. My basic task is to find in every human being the energy that is in them and walk beside them. The purpose of leadership is to create meaningfulness." Siamäk speaks about creativity and creative leadership beautifully, as if it was poetry. He also says that the current organisational structures shackle and hinder creativity. A lot of resources are underused when we only look at the balance sheet and income statement but do not give value to what skills and knowledge the employees have. Creativity can be led in organisations. Diversity brings different views and thoughts through which we gain insights. Some things are culturally bound but others are universal. Therefore, it is very important to get to know not only yourself and your strengths but also the people around you. Trust that everyone has a lot to give. You just need to see them for what they are and they will carry out more than you expected.

Guest writer

SIAMÄK NAGHIAN

CEO, Genelec

Curiosity and creativity are, in my mind, forming the heart of leadership. Leadership is about creativity, innovation and learning how to lead. When you have internalised such a foundation, the other leadership techniques can be built, used and customised based on the needs of people, situations and context.

That is why I have learned to see leadership as a learning, doing, sensation and creation process where the leader and the people are part of the same learning and creating journey. It is about a series of sequences through which different factors help you and the other people to create an unpredictable shared sphere of being.

The essence is the experience of nurturing curiosity, creativity and becoming part of the shared sphere. The most rewarding outcomes are the flourishing of people and the created art. As a leader, I am part of this process where we are looking for something remarkable, and we all bring in what we have learned and experienced for it to become shared, refined, taking us to something new along the way.

6.2 How can I create psychological safety with the people and teams that I work with?

Challenge yourself and your team

I have noticed that there is a certain repeating pattern when you try to drive change in organisations. When you have the creative energy of the change maker, you will, most probably, excite people in the beginning. People will be impressed. You bring a positive breeze of freshness. People want to be in your sphere of influence, and they want your energy, until it starts to frighten them. "Can this influence my role? Can this change the status quo? Can this make me move away from my comfort zone?"

After fear comes resistance; the resistant people will start to put either you or the project down. "This is off. I do not want to be part of this. This is unnecessary. We do not have the time for this…" and so on. Usually the resistant people are also very loud and try to get affirmation and they collect a crowd of critics around them.

ENABLE – BE THE CREATIVE LEADER

Picture 6. The Reaction Process of Creative Ideas Taken into Action

How can you and your team get over that? You need to give it time. Not everyone is as fast paced as you. Not everyone sees the positive impact and the vision as clearly as you do. Communicate. Work with the pioneers. Get results. Demystify the change that you are making. Communicate more. Get more people on the journey with you. Have resilience. Some people will be persistent in their criticism. Others won't want to miss out.

As an enabler, you need to be ready to face resistance. You need to equip yourself and your team with tools to handle the difficulty of the process of change. When they are aware and equipped and do it together, it will eventually feel easy. It is hard to do it alone. Creativity is the embodiment of lightness. The tricky bit is making the change happen, as we live in a world with organisations that are not used to working with people's strengths and thriving with their employees; you will face resistance. Most organisations live by focusing on the bottom line without seeing that the bottom line is very much influenced by the motivation and well-being of the people making the money. If people can use their core skills and feel motivated and valued, companies will thrive along with the people.

> 6.3 How can I equip myself and my team to take the resistance?

You can be the change. And you can bring your creativity to any organisation. It requires patience. It requires belief. And it requires people who will make the change with you. Have a big vision. Be realistic that it will take more time than you would like. Take things forward step by step. Keep the spirit up despite resistance. You can be open about the feelings it raises in you, but you should focus on taking things forward with a good spirit and belief. Remember the target of anabolic energy. It is also important to have some people around you with whom you can vent a bit, to be able to slip to the catabolic side together, being aware of the fact that you cannot stay under the line but need to come back to anabolic energy to get forward. We also need to be able to share the frustration of the moments of despair or feeling stuck. Leadership is, many times, lonely; hence it is critical to always have someone to share your feelings with. Whether it is your fellow leadership team members, some peer group for leaders or your mentor or coach. What are your ways of dealing with the moments of frustration whilst also keeping the focus of the target clear?

6.3.1	How can I equip myself and my team with the resilience to push through despite resistance and delays?
6.3.2	What kind of energy do I bring to the office? First thing, when I come in the morning, while walking in the aisles, whilst interacting in meetings? Do I greet the people, smile, nod? Or do I walk in my thoughts without acknowledging the people around me?

6.3.3 How can I celebrate the successes together with my team?

And when you succeed, celebrate the successes together. Bake a cake for your team and take it to the office. Invite them to your home. Take a walk by the beach and have an ice cream. Have a wintery walk with hot chocolate and a creamy bun. Share a bottle of champagne. Give high fives and have a little dance. Whatever is your way to celebrate, you should do it! At the end of the day, we need to feel the highs to take the lows better. And life is much more fun with celebration. Celebrate often enough. Enjoy what you do.

THE KEY TAKEAWAYS OF CHAPTER 10: ENABLE

In this Chapter you have learned:

- ▶ Creativity is not a heroic myth. It is about doing things together.

- ▶ You do not need to travel around the globe to find the most creative people in the world. You can start from within and then enlarge the circle to the people who surround you.

- ▶ Creativity thrives in surroundings where you do not fear mistakes. Many working cultures do not encourage creativity, but there might be pockets of innovation even within less creative organisations. You can be that change.

- ▶ Since you will be the North Star taking people and teams forward, you carry a lot of responsibility. Make sure you act from a place of anabolic energy, rather than catabolic energy.

- ▶ Today's business world is not about hiding your business ideas and products from your competitors, but instead it is about finding the opportunities to collaborate with different parties. We talk about ecosystems and networks that are created to make an impact together.

CONCLUSIONS: DID YOU CRACK THE CAST?

Congratulations! You have already come far on this journey. I am proud of you for committing to reading this book because it means that you have a strong will to advance yourself as a leader. Even better, if you have done the exercises along the way. Well done you! Going through this process will have helped you define your kind of creativity and become an admired creative leader with anabolic energy. Have you recognised what your spots of ease are? What are your gifts to this world (the areas that you see as so obvious that you did not recognise them before)?

CONCLUSIONS: DID YOU CRACK THE CAST?

The key learnings of this book are that anyone can be creative in their own way and that we can create amazing things when we know ourselves and the people around us. When we connect our different skills and personalities, we can achieve much more together. Creative leadership is not a heroic journey, but instead it is about doing things together. What will you do to take steps forward on this path?

Leaders who are happy to sit in the cast that was formulated for them are people who learned a lot but didn't see the need to develop themselves and their surroundings as they moved forward. Do you feel the urge to crack the cast? I will salute you if you do. The difficulty finding leadership role models that suit you comes from the traditional "masculine" leadership values. Many of the women who made it to the top were using masculine energy even more than the men so they could crack the glass ceiling. To be valued.

I want to be part of creating a different kind of leadership which embraces the strengths and values of each individual. A leadership where we are working together and striving towards mutual respect and win-win solutions.

In a women leaders' event [68]Marja Sakari, the Director of Ateneum art museum in Helsinki, referred to a book by Linda

Nochlin that was called "Why have there been no great women artists?" She said that the book is questioning who defines what is great. In the same way, traditional leadership has been very masculine, as it is traditionally defined: fact and process based and admiring tough leadership. Modern leadership is requiring a balance between masculine and feminine energies and, because of this, what is seen as great leadership is changing. I see that the ethos of leadership is evolving and sensitivity, emotional skills and empathy are rising as skills and features that are valued more and more in leadership. You can be part of defining what is seen as great leadership in the future.

While I was writing this book, there was a debate in the Finnish media and social media about whether it is OK for a leader to cry and show sensitivity. The Finnish Prime Minister Sanna Marin had shed some tears talking about the horrors of the war in Ukraine, and that started a huge debate about whether it was OK for her to show weakness during a crisis. The awkward thing is that she has been criticised before for being too cold and fact based. Many people have come out with comments on where and when they have been crying. Personally, I tend to get tears in my eyes when I am supporting some human being from the bottom of my heart so that they could move forward in their life or in their career. I have always thought that it is true bravery to dare to also show your weak side. We all have different sides to us and that makes us human. I prefer a human being instead of a machine as a leader.

CONCLUSIONS: DID YOU CRACK THE CAST?

The CREATE formula is a demonstration of leadership, with values that are traditionally seen as more feminine: curiosity, empathy, collaboration, creating together, understanding of different personalities, communication and enabling. At the same time, it is good to have the processes in place to be able to get space for creativity. You do not need to be a woman or feel like a woman to lead from the CREATE perspective, but you do need to have values that are aligned with them. A lot of people do not want to work at the cost of their health, families and spare time, regardless of their gender. More and more people strive towards sustainable success: A success that is sustainable for both the individuals and the organisation, as well as for nature.

If you have enjoyed the book and it feels like you learned something new about yourself and creative leadership, before you put it down, try to identify what the key learnings were for you that will help you to crack the cast and act as the genuine you. What people really want from you is to be seen for who they are and to be respected for that. If you are open and vulnerable about your strengths and weaknesses, the people around you will dare to do that too. You have the responsibility to create the psychological safety required to try, fail and learn. The better you recognise your strengths and development areas, the better you can use your personality traits in leadership and creativity.

Notice in your surroundings the people who tend to put down creative ideas and efforts. How can you make a change in your organisation by supporting the people who have a lot of ideas so that they do not feel defeated and ignored? How can you listen to the voices that might not be heard, and invite ideas from people who do not speak up so easily? I remind you to stand up for innovative initiatives. They might not get through as such, but they can be expanded further in collaboration. The usual comment is that we shouldn't change things for the sake of change. There needs to be a purpose and a valid reason for the planned actions of change, but sometimes the reason may be hard to define. How can you challenge the ideas in a way that is positive and forward-looking and gives the people a feeling of being heard and respected? An important reflection to complete when developing organisations is how the planned action influences the client experience and the employee experience.

My notion from numerous organisations is that, even if creativity and innovation are set as important strategic targets, innovative and creative ideas are not always being respected. What can you do in your surroundings to give creativity the value it deserves? The best thing is to be vocal about it. Be proud of your own kind of creativity and praise your team members and collaboration partners for their innovative ideas. Support the people around you to find their approach to creativity. Give this book to someone who you think would benefit from it.

The more people start to embrace their creativity, the more the world we live in will not only become more fun and interesting but also more tolerant and psychologically safe. If it becomes the norm to operate with your strengths rather than through learned patterns and presumed values, we will all be able to breathe more lightly. We live in a world with so many struggles, worries and catastrophes that everything that can bring feelings of success through ease and respect makes the world a better place. While crafting the CREATE road map, I learned a lot about myself, and I felt that it increased my self-confidence. I was reminded of my strengths and started to see more light and colours around me again. It was a very powerful and energising process for me. I hope this formula will help you on your path too.

Maybe my stories resonated with you, or maybe you got yourself some tool that you use in your everyday life or leadership. I hope I have inspired you to see that anything is possible with the right attitude. You are the change, and you can have a huge impact on your surroundings.

As you have read this far, I am sure you share with me my passion for creativity and leadership and see the benefits of combining these two areas. Are you ready to practise active listening? Will you ask open questions of your team members or other people you work with so that you can hear how you can move forward as a creative team?

I am asking you three final questions that will help you to map out where you stand, and to set out some targets for your journey as a creative leader:

1. What does creative leadership mean to me? Map your learnings from the book.

2. What am I going to do within the next three months to develop myself as a creative leader?

3. How will I make sure that I do not bounce back to the cast that I am being put in, but proudly represent myself as the creative leader that I am?

If you like the stories and ideas that I have presented, there are plenty of ways we can work together. The book gives a set of tools for you, but you can look much more deeply into the subject going forward.

You can find the CREATE workbook at www.fastcreative.ninja/workbook/. You can learn about my coaching, and how I am also available for public speaking. The offering may change with time, but the intention remains the same.

You can find the latest information on my website.

Looking forward to hearing about your contribution towards creative leadership. This is a movement, and the input of all of us is significant in creating a revolution of creative leadership. We will be powerful together. Crack the cast and spray the creative energy around you. Thank you for being on this journey with me.

Maija

WWW.LINKEDIN.COM/IN/MAIJA-FAST-9554534/

WWW.FASTCREATIVE.NINJA

A HUMBLE THANK YOU TO MY CREATIVE FAMILY

I want to thank my family for being the inspiration for this book: My grandmother Eeva, who had full confidence that I could do anything in my life. My parents, Pia and Harri, for their big love and unwavering trust. Thank you for creating a safe space for me to evolve, grow and experiment. You showed and taught me creativity and the value of it. My sister, Stiina, who is an inspirational example of always creating something and getting things done.

My father drew with us, my parents sewed clothes for me and my sister together, we went to museums and to art school. Our home was full of art and books. As an architect, my father used to redesign our home together with my mother every couple of years, and the house lived and changed based on our needs at the time. My parents have also been great entertainers for their grandchildren and created a magical happy place for us in the Finnish archipelago, a place where the children and their needs were the initiators for the design.

My father really has an eye for opportunities to be creative and he is very inspirational in his capability to ideate, draw and implement. He builds houses, creates interiors, details and landscapes. My mother stands by him in every project and helps him. She is the one who makes time for the children, and she finds endless joy in being with them and listening to them. Her laughter chimes and carries far.

I also want to thank my other Carelian grandmother, Ulla, who never had the chance to use her talents for herself. That was the spirit of the time. Women could not fulfil their dreams and use their abilities. Instead, she gave all her four boys dolls of their own. She taught her sons to sew and knit clothes for their dolls. They all had their tiny irons (which were actually made of iron back then) and they learned to iron the clothes of their dolls. They learned to clean and to cook. That was not common at the beginning of the 1950s. My grandmother raised boys of tomorrow.

Her husband, my other Swedish Finnish grandfather, Gunnar, was a silversmith and carpenter. He was a very handy man and taught his sons to create and to build. Gunnar was a very well-liked man, and he was always ready to help others. I can still hear his warm laughter years after his death.

Grandpa Nils was also a funny, humorous man and he taught us an entrepreneurial mindset. I am grateful to my uncle Nils-Erik (Puppe) and his wife Lena for giving me the chance to do a trainee period in their architect bureau to familiarise myself with working life when I was 15. And thank you cousins Katja and Jonna for all our arts experiences together.

I grew up surrounded by people who were creative in different ways, and I want to give that to my children too. I want to make everyday life an adventure. We create parties on normal days, print T-shirts, paint with berries, organise events, go to art museums and welcome friends to our home. We go swimming or flying in a wind tube or to an escape room or have breakfast in the woods. Our children have become very good at creating a beautiful party table for a barbecue in the garden on a normal evening. Everyone is playing along and doing their little bit. Special thanks should be given to my inspirational children, who make life so much more interesting.

Ebba, 10, is the most creative person I have met. She inspires me with her endless capability to change and with her interior design skills that she shows when she is redesigning her room almost every week. She has created a company and sells her own handmade jewellery. She makes things happen with her tiny, strong body and creative mind. She stands more on her hands than on her feet and has a phenomenal eye for colour. She is just brilliant and radiates love, empathy and delicate power.

Eelis, 12, used to spontaneously launch into handicrafts at eight o'clock in the morning when he was four years old.

Until today, his speciality has been to make magic from boxes. I admire Eelis's natural leadership skills, which I have had the pleasure to follow, both on the football field and off it. It is amazing how much creative leadership football can teach. Eelis takes others into consideration and encourages especially those who are weaker at something. Eelis gets easily into any team or activity. He is a very talented, fair and lovable boy who feels strongly for justice.

Oliver, 14, my bonus son, has been exposed to the creativity in our family since he was 6 and suddenly, at the age of 12, found the creativity in himself big time, starting to draw, to make colourful lures and to crochet baskets. And when he did – he got very into it. Oliver digs deep into things, just like his father. I am so proud of how he has taken in the creativity and started to make things of his own.

The children are all very different and have their own set of traits and skills. The best thing is when they put their heads together and work on something together. The other day they started to create shoes from shoebox cardboard and designed a colourful logo together, along with a shop and a website for their newly launched cardboard shoe company. Creative leadership is about bringing different people and skills together to create something new. I am happy that our children can learn from each other and their different strengths at home.

Last but not least, I want to thank my partner, Guy, who always encourages me to embrace my inspiration and to trust my intuition. He has been incredibly supportive during the process of writing this book, even letting me write quite a lot about his life and career despite being introverted and not being naturally inclined to tell his story as loudly. Guy sees me the way no one else does. He listens to me, believes in my ideas and implements things together with me. He is an endless inspiration in how he has used rough experiences from the past as a driving force for creating good. Guy had a belief that he was not creative, but with me, he found out that he actually is very imaginative and has an eye for beauty. And I love it when he listens to comedy while cooking us delicious meals, laughing out loud all the while.

Thank you Guy for enabling my book project and for sharing life with me.

MEET THE AUTHOR

Maija Fast is an enabler, catalyst and connector. She brings creativity to business, seeking opportunities everywhere by developing innovative leadership skills and helping to promote an open mindset in organisations. Maija is an experienced HR Director, Certified Business Coach, Author and Entrepreneur on a path to changing the world.

Maija has been described by her friends and colleagues as always having many colourful butterflies in the air. She is a bubbly and energetic personality who inspires and engages the people around her. She has been said to get the best out of people and to make them visible.

Maija is an inspiring event organiser, gallerist and public speaker. Maija has brought colour and communality to her neighbourhood. She has moved statues, organised events and brought people together to create previously unseen experiences. The biggest events she organised were two Children's Dream events with thousands of participants. She has brought together passionate people with different skillsets in her violin shop gallery. She has exhibited the art of several female photo artists, ceramists and painters. She has been invited to speak at international seminars, events and university lecture series. Her passion is to support people and organisations to thrive.

Maija has held several leadership roles, been part of seven leadership teams and has led associations and open networks. She has worked for more than 20 years in multiple fields and organisations internationally, and she has seen different leadership and communication styles. She is in search of the perfect organisation culture. Maija inspires individuals, organisations and open networks to think outside the box and innovate. She believes that success comes through seeing the strengths of people and building teams with complementary skills and motivators. Maija knows that people who are respected want to give their best, and teams who have fun together get results. Work that feels enjoyable is successful.

Maija is a Certified Business Coach (ICF) and she has been coaching individuals and leading coaching programmes in many organisations as well as with her Fast Creative company. As a coach, she focuses on listening and supporting the coachee to find their kind of creativity and their own path. She sees herself as an enabler of growth. She can help her clients find new sides of themselves and notice the elements that are within that are too obvious to notice on your own.

Maija grew up in a family where creativity was valued, and this is exactly what she wants to offer to her children and other people around her. She is a mother of children with an innovative outlook: a son and a daughter and a bonus son. She enjoys following her children's progress, seeing them grow up with different personalities and different kinds of creativity. She sees creativity as something much broader than how it is usually defined. It can be expressed with different forms of art, but it is not only art. It is a mindset.

In 2015, Maija was nominated as the Most Positive Citizen of Helsinki. You would never be bored with Maija. She wants to make everyday life an adventure. Any average evening is a possibility for a barbecue in the garden, lockdown limitations end up with a family party in a limousine and, for her fortieth birthday, she organised a colour carnival with her partner. One of her favourite things is taking a morning swim. She loves dancing and delicious food, and she also likes to cosy up in front of the fireplace with a glass of good wine.

You can find more information about Maija's work on www.fastcreative.ninja

BIBLIOGRAPHY

Amabile, Teresa M.: How to Kill Creativity. On Creativity, Harvard Business Review's must reads, Harvard Business Review Publishing, 2021.

Bourke, Juliet & Titus Andrea: Why Inclusive Leaders Are Good For Organisations, and How To Become One, Harvard Business Review, 3/2019.

Brown, Brené: Atlas of the Heart. Mapping Meaningful Conversations and the Language of Human Experience, Penguin Random House, 2021.

Brown, Brené: Dare to Lead, Rohkaiseva johtaja, Viisas Elämä, 2019.

Byron Katie: Loving What Is, Harmony Books, New York.

Deloitte: Human Capital Trends. The rise of the social enterprise, Deloitte Insights, 2018.

Doyle, Glennon: Untamed. Stop Pleasing, Start Living, Penguin Random House UK, 2020.

Elsbach, Kimberly D., Brown-Saracino, Brooke & Flynn, Francis J.: Collaborating with Creative Peers. Harvard Business Review's must reads. Harvard Business Review Publishing, 2021.

Gino, Francesca: The Business Case for Curiosity. On Creativity, Harvard Business Review's must reads. Harvard Business Review Publishing, 2021.

Hamel, Gary & Zanini, Michele: Humanocracy: Creating Organisations as Amazing as People Inside Them, Harvard Business Review. Boston, Massachusetts, 2020.

Heer, Dain Dr: Being you. Changing the World, 2011.

Joiner, Bill: A Leadership Agility: a Global Imperative, Dialogue, 2014.

Lencione, Patrick: The Five Dysfunctions of a Team. Kindle.

Maister, David H.: True Professionalism. The Courage to Care About Your People, Your Clients and Your Career, Touchstone, New York, 2000.

Parker, Priya: The Art of Gathering: How We Meet and Why it Matters, Kindle.

Pölönen, Perttu: Tulevaisuuden lukujärjestys, Otava, 2021.

Raami, Asta: Älykäs intuitio ja miten me käytämme sitä, Kustantamo S&S, 2016.

Rahkamo Susanna & Valpas Pauliina: Luova työ 2030, Yellow Method.

Rinne, April: FLUX, Kindle.

Ruuska, Inkeri: Moniosaamisen renesanssi. Opas työelämän edelläkävijöille, Basam Books, 2022.

Suomalaisen Työn liitto/The Association for Finnish work: Työntekijä- ja työnantajakysely, 2016.

Tuominen, Camilla: Tunteet ei kuulu työpaikalle, Otava, 2020.

Webb, Caroline: How to Have a Good Day. Think Bigger, Feel Better and Transform Your Working Life. Pan Macmillan, 2016.

KEYNOTES AND SEMINARS

Bregman, Rutger: Time for a New View of Human Nature, Nordic Business Forum 20.9.2022.

Edmondson, Amy: The Fearless Organisation. Building a culture of psychological safety to thrive in an uncertain world, Nordic Business Forum 2022.

Kilpinen, Paula: Sankarijohtajasta strategiseksi ihmisjohtajaksi. Keynote, MySpeaker LeadersHub, 11.11.22.

Kramer, Jitske: Building A Future-Proof Coporate Culture, Nordic Business Forum, 20.9.2022.

Naghian, Siamäk: The Leadership Forum for Creativity and Innovation, Work 2030 programme. Seminar 19.1.2022.

Sakari, Marja: Women's network: Paving the Way for Leadership & Inspiration, Amcham and Ateneum, Seminar 16.3.2022.

Tuominen, Camilla: Workplace emotions & wise encounters with customers, Keynote at Bird & Bird, 2022.

TRAINING

Backman, Heli & Karlsson, Nina: Energy Leader Trainer® Programme and course book, Energy Coaching, 2022.

Backman, Heli & Karlsson, Nina: Lawyer Leadership Programme and course book, Energy Coaching, 2022.

PODCASTS

Leading Energy: hosts Heli Backman & Nina Karlsson.

Nordic Leaders: Guest Patricia Ryan Madson, hosts Nick Vertigans, David Goddard & Stefano Mosconi.

OTHER

Brown, Brené: The Power of Vulnerability, TED talk on YouTube.
https://www.ted.com/talks/brene_brown_the_power_of_vulnerability
19.4.2022

Divergent thinking Ken Robinson's paperclip test:
https://www.dailymotion.com/video/x2pva29
17.7.2022

Henri Alén's strategy price:
https://www.ssjs.fi/?x103997=650424
16.4.2022

Minna Parikka's words: Pupujen paluu. Stockmann 160, The Official Guide 2022.

ENDNOTES

1. Brown on Facebook, March 31 2018
2. Edmondson: The Fearless Organisation
3. Syvärinen: Taikaelämää (Instagram) – Free translation from Finnish, approved by Katri Syvärinen
4. Camilla Tuominen: Tunteet eivät kuulu työpaikalle
5. Perttu Pölönen: Tulevaisuuden lukujärjestys
6. Amabile: How to Kill Creativity
7. Edmondson: The Fearless Organisation
8. Hamel and Zanini: Humanocracy. Creating Organisations as Amazing as People Inside Them
9. Human Capital Trends. The rise of the social enterprise
10. Doyle: Untamed. Stop Pleasing, Start Living
11. Bregman: Time for a New View of Human Nature
12. The Association for Finnish work: Employee and employer survey (Työntekijä- ja työnantajakysely)
13. Dr. Heer: Being you. Changing the world
14. Dr. Heer: Being you. Changing the world
15. Song by Helen Elise Austin Lyrics © Pigfactory Usa LLC
16. Song by Chris Martin / Will Champion / Guy Berryman / Andrew Taggart / Johnny Buckland Lyrics © Universal Music Publishing Mgb Ltd., Sony/atv Allegro, Nice Hair Publishing
17. Brown on Facebook, March 31 2018
18. Song by Christopher Porter, Peter Gordeno, Howard New
19. Joiner: A Leadership Agilty: a Global Imperative
20. Madson in Nordic Leadership podcast
21. Rinne: FLUX
22. Ruuska: Moniosaamisen renesanssi. Opas työelämän edelläkävijöille
23. Pölönen: Tulevaisuuden lukujärjestys

24	Rahkamo and Valpas: Luova työ 2030
25	Rahkamo and Valpas: Creative Work 2030
26	Hären: MySpeaker Keynote about Creativity
27	Song by Alex Kapranos. Lyrics © Universal Music Publishing Group
28	Rahkamo and Valpas: Creative Work 2030
29	Gino: The Business Case for Curiosity
30	Parikka: Stockmann 160
31	Raami: Älykäs intuitio ja miten me käytämme sitä
32	Song by: Bonnie Leigh McKee / Henry Walter / Katy Perry / Lukasz Gottwald / Max Martin.Lyrics © Concord Music Publishing LLC, Kobalt Music Publishing Ltd., Warner Chappell Music, Inc
33	Elsbach, Brown-Saracino and Flynn: Collaborating with Creative Peers
34	Rahkamo and Valpas: Creative Work 2030
35	Kilpinen: Sankarijohtajasta strategiseksi ihmisjohtajaksi
36	Brown: Atlas of the Heart
37	Tuominen: Workplace emotions & wise encounters with customers
38	Song by Lionel Richie. Lyrics © Sony/ATV Music Publishing LLC
39	Raami: Älykäs intuitio ja miten me käytämme sitä
40	Dr. Heer: Being you and changing the world
41	Maister: True professionalism
42	Dr Heer: Being you. Changing the World
43	Dr Heer: Being you. Changing the World
44	Edmondson: The Fearless Organisation
45	Dr Heer: Being you. Changing the world
46	Byron Katie: Loving what is
47	Kramer: Building a Future-Proof Corporate Culture
48	Song by Bob Marley Lyrics © Universal Music Publishing Group
49	Webb: How To Have a Good Day
50	Brown: Dare to Lead
51	Brown: e.g. The Power of Vulnerability TedEX talk, Dare to Lead, Atlas of the Heart
52	Webb: How to Have a Good Day
53	Brown: TED talk The Power of Vulnerability

54 Song by Greg Kurstin / Sia Furler / Will Gluck Lyrics © Ole Media Management Lp, Sony/ATV Music Publishing LLC, Warner Chappell Music, Inc
55 Lencione: The Five Dysfunctions of a Team
56 Rahkamo and Valpas: Creative Work 2030
57 Parker: The Art of Gathering
58 Song by Eric Clapton Lyrics © Warner/Chappell Music International Ltd., Eric Patrick Clapton, E C Music Ltd
59 Deloitte: Human Capital Trends. The rise of the social enterprise.
60 Sinek on Twitter, February 18 2022
61 Webb: How to Have a Good Day
62 Backman and Karlsson: Energy Coaching, Energy Leader Trainer®
63 Webb: How to Have a Good Day
64 Backman and Karlsson: Energy Leader Trainer® Programme
65 Amabile: How To Kill Creativity
66 Houttu: Presentation at the MySpeaker and Nordic Business Forum speaker contest
67 Naghian: The Leadership Forum for Creativity and Innovation, Work 2030
68 Sakari: Women's Network: Paving the Way for Leadership & Inspiration

www.ingramcontent.com/pod-product-compliance
Lightning Source LLC
Chambersburg PA
CBHW072045110526
44590CB00018B/3047